Clothed with Power

A Brief Study of
the Indwelling of
the Holy Spirit

Also by GARY CAGE

The Holy Spirit: A Sourcebook with Commentary

Clothed with Power

A Brief Study of the Indwelling of the Holy Spirit

Gary T. Cage

CHARLOTTE HOUSE PUBLISHERS
RENO, NEVADA

Copyright © 1996 by Charlotte House Publishers
P. O. Box 50147
Reno, Nevada 89503-0147
All rights reserved
Printed in the United States

ISBN# 0-9654828-0-4

To Zachary, Charles, and Caleb

My son, if your heart is wise,
    my heart too will be glad.
My soul will rejoice
    when your lips speak what is right.

Proverbs 23.15-16

TABLE OF CONTENTS

Acknowledgments	8
Introduction	9
Chapter One: The Holy Spirit in the Old Testament	12
Chapter Two: The Spirit of God in Jewish Intertestamental and Secular Graeco-Roman Literature	23
Chapter Three: The Holy Spirit in Matthew and Mark	36
Chapter Four: The Holy Spirit in Luke and Acts	46
Chapter Five: The Holy Spirit in the Writings of John	65
Chapter Six: The Holy Spirit in Hebrews, I-II Peter, and Jude	86
Chapter Seven: The Holy Spirit in the Letters of Paul	96
Chapter Eight: Conclusions	123

ACKNOWLEDGMENTS

I began my studies on the Holy Spirit about twenty-five years ago. During that time my wife and I have been involved in the raising of three sons, several foreign missionary endeavors and church ministries in the United States, and I have been privileged to teach philosophy at the University of Nevada, Reno. My family especially has been so very encouraging to me in my studies, but I have another family as well, the church of which I am a member here in Reno. It was the latter who encouraged me to develop my class notes on the Holy Spirit into a book, a project which became *The Holy Spirit, A Sourcebook with Commentary*, published just last year. Then, several people in various parts of the country encouraged me to produce a synopsis of the work so that more people might be able to examine my thesis. Hence, this present book.

I am grateful to all of the people just mentioned, but especially to Rick Warren and Stan Paher, who have taken a special interest in this project. Stan has provided me primarily with invaluable technical advice with regard to the production of books, and Rick has helped me, not only with ideas relating to the issue of the Holy Spirit in the Bible, but also with encouragement with regard to writing this second book on the subject. I should add two others to this special list. David Phillips, a long time friend, who, though he did not suggest this book, has helped me so very much with his willingness to discuss these issues from time to time. And finally, I thank Dr. William Hunter, who has reminded me once again how important it is to be dedicated to a pursuit of the truth.

INTRODUCTION

This little volume is an abridgment of my earlier work, *The Holy Spirit: A Sourcebook with Commentary* (referred to hereafter as *The Sourcebook*). In that work I set out as much of the background material I possibly could to the New Testament writers' use of the relevant terms having to do with the Holy Spirit. I included every pertinent passage from the Old Testament and as many excerpts which I could find in the Dead Sea Scrolls, the Talmud, the Aramaic Targums, Jewish apocalyptic literature, as well as the writings of Philo and Josephus. I also included as part of the background excerpts from Zoroastrian, Greek, and Roman literature which had to do with divine spirits, especially as these spirits indwelled human beings. Having collated my general conclusions, I went on to interpret the New Testament statements on the Holy Spirit.

The problems with this approach were several. The work itself is a bit unwieldy for the general Bible student. The effort to provide as many references as possible made the work repetitious. The collation of the material was tedious. The copious references to current scholars' opinions footnoted in the text are not of great interest to the average reader. And finally, the work assumed much too great a familiarity with background materials.

So, in the pages which follow I will reduce the findings of the bigger book to just those which are the most direct and relevant. I devote one chapter to the OT, one chapter to all the non-canonical background material, and then I divide up the remaining chapters among the NT writers; my main concern is the interpretation of the NT passages on the Holy Spirit.

The nature and function of the Holy Spirit according to the Bible is a very popular topic these days. (In another book I would like to discuss why this is so, but it is a fact nonetheless.) I have a main thesis which I think is borne out by the evidence: that when the biblical writers referred to the indwelling of the Holy Spirit they could have meant only one thing, namely, miraculous powers, and especially prophecy. For a Christian disciple to have the Spirit of God dwelling in him meant that he had been gifted by God with one or more of several miraculous powers, most notably the gift of prophetic utterance.

Before beginning our brief survey of the relevant data, I wish to make a few comments about literary interpretation, and biblical interpretation in particular. It should go without saying that our first concern is to discover the historical context of a passage in order to discern accurately what was the intended message of the original author to his particular audience. It is simply improper to read modern concerns into an ancient text. We also need to practice restraint in the face of ambiguity. Commonly an author will leave himself open to more than one possible interpretation; it is the modern reader's *duty* at this point to recognize the multiple possibilities without forcing the data into a desired configuration. However, equally commonly are those occasions when the author makes himself very clear. These are the passages which should fix our doctrine. We should then rely upon the unambiguous passages to interpret the ambiguous ones.

With these things in mind we proceed to our survey. In *The Sourcebook* I focused on passages which used the respective words for "spirit" in connection with God. Those words in their respective languages can mean many other things, such as breath, wind, mind, attitude, demon, courage, anger, and can be associated with things other than God, such as humans, animals and even inanimate nature, but when used in connection with God I found ninety-seven relevant passages in the OT, passages where spirit is associated with God. So to these we now turn.

CHAPTER ONE

THE HOLY SPIRIT IN THE OLD TESTAMENT

In the 97 passages in the OT which connect the Spirit with God we find that by far the most oft-used phrase is "the Spirit of the Lord," while "the Holy Spirit" occurs only twice (Ps. 51.11 and Is. 63.10-11). In connection with a person, though, we find quite a few interchangeable expressions:
- the Spirit in a person,
- being filled with the Spirit,
- being clothed with the Spirit,
- receiving the outpouring of the Spirit,
- the Spirit falling upon someone, and
- being stirred by the Spirit.

However, from the contexts it appears that no significant distinctions emerge from this group of phrases.

Overall in the OT God's Spirit implies His power, and whenever we find the Spirit of the Lord in connection with a human being the result is miracle-working power. In the 97 passages we find 163 occurrences of the Spirit in connection with God. Forty-six of these are quite clearly not God's Spirit as an active entity in its own right. Most are anthropomorphic references to God's breath. Some are actually winds sent by God, and some are references to God's mind, as in, for example, God's Spirit made impatient, or God's Spirit being omnipresent. There are 30 instances of God's Spirit as some kind of active entity indwelling a person, and in each case there is an indication of some kind of miraculous activity, such as prophecy, revelations, or extraordinary acts of power.

Another way to look at this issue is to see how often the miraculous clearly plays a part in spirit occurrences, even in those instances where it is questionable as to whether it is God's Spirit in reference. Of the 163 examples considered in my earlier work, *The Sourcebook*, 57 clearly involve the miraculous and another 38 probably do for a total of 95. Now, one needs to remember at this point that many of the passages are silent. They might involve the miraculous and they might not. None of the contexts of the passages which are about the Spirit of God indwelling a person would exclude the miraculous. So, if we let the clear statements interpret the ambiguous ones, it would seem that the general use of the phrase "the Spirit of the Lord" in the OT was to indicate the possession of miraculous powers.

Let us look at some examples. Our first one is Nu. 11.16-30, which continued to play an important role in the Jewish understanding of the Holy Spirit down through the centuries. In Nu. 11 we find Moses despairing over the recalcitrant attitude of the Israelites he had led out into the wilderness. So, God responded by ordering Moses to select seventy elders and officers of the people to stand with him at the tent of meeting. "Then the Lord came down in the cloud and spoke to him, and took some of the spirit that was upon him and put it upon the seventy elders; and when the spirit rested upon them, they prophesied" (vs. 25, Revised Standard Version). An interesting aspect of this story concerns Eldad and Medad, two of the seventy elders yet two men who had not gone to the tent with the others. The "spirit rested upon them" also, and they too prophesied. Some complained about it, but Moses responded, "Are you jealous for my sake? Would that all the Lord's people were prophets, that the Lord would put his spirit upon them!" (vs. 29). In this story there is not only the unmistakable connection between the indwelling Spirit and prophecy, but there is also some indication of a measuring of the Spirit, that is, "some" of the Spirit which was upon Moses was given to the seventy. As I have already stated, this story developed into an expectation that one day (in the day of the Messiah) God would bestow His Spirit on all His people, not just upon the leaders.

Another story of far-reaching influence for Jewish theologians was the story of Balaam in Nu. 22-24. Balaam was a Moabite who was known for his oracular powers, though they most probably were not genuine. Balak, the king of Moab, sought to pay Balaam for his services, hoping for a curse upon the Israelites. Surprisingly, God indeed spoke to Balaam, telling him not to go to the king. Apparently Balaam wanted the king's money and was finally allowed by God to go prophesy, but on the way God impressed upon Balaam the importance of speaking truthfully by causing his beast to speak to him and also by revealing to Balaam a vision of God's angel dressed in warrior's garb. God then sent His Spirit upon Balaam, causing him to prophesy in favor of the Israelites. Later, in Nu. 31.16, Balaam is assigned impure motives and implicated in a scheme to thwart the Israelites' progress, a fact which was taken by the rabbis later to explain why the Gentiles had had the Holy Spirit and prophecy taken away from them.

In the next section of the OT we come to Joshua, who is also said to have received the Spirit (Dt. 34.9-12). The same is said of many of the judges, Othniel (Ju. 3.7-10), Gideon (Ju. 6.33-35), Jephthah (Ju. 11.29-40), and especially Samson. Samson's story is a case of one's progressively receiving the Spirit of the Lord upon him, resulting in his famous mighty deeds (Ju. 13.24-25, 14.5-6, 14.19, 15.14-15).

However, one of the most interesting cases is that of King Saul. The bashful Saul had the Spirit of God to come upon him with the result that he prophesied. In his case it appears that prophecy overpowered him, putting him in a trance-like state (I Sm. 10.1-16). He also was empowered as a leader of God's people (I Sm. 11.5-7). However, as the story goes, Saul became insanely jealous of the young David and sought to kill the latter. God's Spirit then departed Saul, "and an evil spirit from the Lord tormented him" (I Sm. 16.14).

David, though, serves as an encouraging contrast to Saul. David began to be filled with the Spirit of the Lord upon his being anointed (I Sm. 16.13) with at least one result being prophetic powers. "The Spirit of the Lord speaks by me, his word is upon my tongue," David said (II Sm. 23.2). As we all know, David sinned in many ways, the most famous being the murder of Uriah and adultery with Bathsheba, but unlike Saul, David repented in utter contrition with his profound sentiments being captured in the fifty-first psalm.

> Behold, thou desirest truth in the inward being;
> therefore teach me wisdom in my secret heart.
> [7]Purge me with hyssop, and I shall be clean;
> Wash me and I shall be whiter than snow.
> [8]Fill me with joy and gladness;
> Let the bones which thou hast broken rejoice.
> [9]Hide thy face from my sins,
> and blot out my iniquities.
> [10]Create in me a new heart, O God,
> and put a new and right spirit within me.
> [11]Cast me not away from thy presence,
> and take not thy holy Spirit from me.
> [12]Restore to me the joy of thy salvation,
> and uphold me with a willing spirit.
> [13]Then I will teach transgressors thy ways,
> and sinners will return to thee.
> [14]Deliver me from bloodguiltiness,
> O God, thou God of my salvation,
> and my tongue will sing aloud of thy deliverance.

> ⁱ⁷The sacrifice acceptable to God is a broken spirit;
> a broken and contrite heart, O God, thou wilt not despise.

A well-known feature of Hebrew poetry is its parallelism, where the lines of a couplet express the same idea twice. This feature is quite evident in Ps. 51. Notice how "spirit" is used interchangeably with "heart" (vv. 10 and 17), which is equivalent to the inner man (vs. 6). David wanted God to change him on the inside, and from the context it could be said that this change could apparently be effected by forgiveness. As for the phrase in vs. 11: "take not thy holy spirit from me," we can take it in the sense that David feared the removal of the Spirit of God as in the all too familiar case of Saul, or, given the Jewish poetic parallelism in vs. 11, having God's holy spirit would be the same as having God's presence, or God's fellowship, not a matter of indwelling. (Linguistically, there is no way to distinguish between "your holy spirit" and "the spirit of your holiness.") Of course, both meanings could be there: David worried about the loss of prophetic inspiration and the sense of closeness to God that that gift provided.

Yet another interesting case is the story of Elijah and Elisha. Elijah as a prophet was directed by the Spirit as to how to elude King Ahab (I K. 18.12). Moreover, at the end of his life Elisha asked Elijah for a double share of his spirit, needed of course to carry on the prophetic ministry. He received it and began a series of fascinating miracles. Another thing that is interesting in this story is that God's Spirit, as an indwelling source of power and inspiration, is referred to as Elijah's spirit, a point to which we shall return when we examine some NT passages.

Some interesting data with regard to the Holy Spirit come also from the Book of Isaiah. For example, we find the following in chapter 11.

> ¹There shall come forth a shoot from the stump of Jesse, a branch shall grow out of his roots.
> ²And the Spirit of the Lord shall rest upon him,
>   the spirit of wisdom and understanding,
>   the spirit of counsel and might,
>   the spirit of knowledge and the fear of the Lord.
> ³And his delight shall be in the fear of the Lord.

The context (10.5-12.6) has to do with Assyria, the rod of God's wrath, itself to be punished in due time. The figure of the defoliation of a forest is used throughout. The point is that the Davidic line (cf. I Sm. 7.8-16), like a shoot beside a dead stump, would survive the current judgment upon Israel and that there would arise a king who would rule with a spiritual perspective (poetically overstated). This future Davidic king would enjoy the Spirit of the Lord resting upon him, resulting in wisdom, understanding, diplomacy, strength, knowledge and respect for God. This possession of the Spirit should most probably be understood to be of the type enjoyed by other leaders in the past, for example, Moses, Joshua, the judges, Saul and David. (In fact, I was surprised to find such broad agreement among the scholars that Is. 11.2 is describing charismata of the Spirit, such things as prophecy and revelations, which were seen as essential requirements for one to be an Israelite leader.)

Another different but equally interesting reference from Isaiah comes from 31.3, where Isaiah chastised his countrymen for relying upon Egypt's military rather than upon God's wisdom: "The Egyptians are men, and not God; and their horses are flesh, and not spirit." This is the first clear contrast in the Bible between flesh and spirit. This is no reference to the Holy Spirit, rather it makes spirit an essential characteristic of God.

Another contribution by Isaiah is the metaphor of the outpouring of the Spirit. In 32.12-19 Isaiah predicted the transformation of Palestine into a desert as a punishment for unrighteousness. However, one day, Isaiah says, "the Spirit (will be) poured out upon us from on high," and just as water converts a desert into an oasis, Israel would again become a place of righteousness. We find similar language in 44.3-4:

> For I will pour water on the thirsty land, and streams on the dry ground. I will pour my Spirit upon your descendants, and my blessing on your offspring. They shall spring up like grass amid waters, like willows by flowing streams.

Whatever Isaiah meant by the outpouring of the Spirit, it signified the return of God's good favor.

Finally, in Isaiah and his contemporaries we find the usual equation between possessing the Spirit and being a prophet. Isaiah claimed to have the Spirit and to have been anointed to go preach good news to the people (61.1-4, cf. 48.16, 59.21). Hosea bemoaned the bad attitude of the people toward God's spokesmen, "The prophet is a fool, the man of the spirit is mad, . . ." (9.7). Micah also claimed to have the Spirit as a prophet (3.7-8).

Moving on to the next century, we come to Ezekiel, who provides some very unusual facets to our study. Much of the book recounts Ezekiel's visions from the Lord. In two visions the Spirit enters Ezekiel and stands him upon his feet (2.2, 3.24). In others Ezekiel is lifted up as if flying (3.12-14, 8.3, 11.1, 24, 37.1, 43.4-5). And again, the Spirit enters Ezekiel and gives him a prophetic message to deliver to the people (11.5).

However, the most unusual passages have to do with promises of a future indwelling of a spirit. God, promising to bring the people back from captivity, says (11.19-20),

> And I will give them one heart, and put a new spirit within them; I will take the stony heart out of their flesh, [20]that they may walk in my statutes and keep my ordinances and obey them; and they shall be my people, and I will be their God.

Similarly, Ezk. 36. 26-27:

> A new heart I will give you, and a new spirit I will put within you; and I will take out of your flesh the heart of stone and give you a heart of flesh. [27]And I will put my spirit within you, and cause you to walk in my statutes and be careful to observe my ordinances.

Of all the references we find in the OT to the Holy Spirit these last two appear most to indicate that the function of the indwelling Spirit is moral, empowering one for obedience, yet there are problems with that conclusion. First of all, it is quite clear that Ezekiel meant the same thing by "spirit" as he does by "heart". It was a reference to a new attitude, one of obedience. Neither was that attitude given directly by God, since Ezekiel is very strong on individual human responsibility (cf. chapter 18). Even here Ezekiel warned those who would refuse to take on this heart of obedience that they would receive God's judgment upon them (11.21). Evidently, Ezekiel meant that as a result of the destruction of Jerusalem and the consequent exile that future children of Israel would be more responsive to God's law. In that sense God could be said to have given them a new spirit, not a stony spirit but His spirit, that is, a spirit acquiescent to God's will. Elsewhere in Ezekiel God effects a change in His people through sword and exile (6.8-10), through the disastrous consequences of listening to false prophets (14.1-11), by forgiving them freely and restoring them to Palestine (20.40-44), and by giving them a new Davidic shepherd over a united Israel (37.23-28). So, God's spirit is not the *cause* of Israel's repentance, rather it is the *same thing* as their repentance. This is further corroborated by the parallel passage of Ezk. 18.31, in which the Jews are told to get for themselves a new heart and a new spirit so as to avoid punishment. All of this would seem to indicate that God's spirit in these passages was a new attitude mediated through circumstances rather than through the Holy Spirit. (Incidentally, Jewish interpreters do not see these verses as references to the Holy Spirit, as neither do the RSV translators.)

Finally, the fifth century writers consistently referred to Spirit-possession as the power to prophesy. Nehemiah said that God had given His good Spirit to instruct His people (9.20), by which he meant that He had warned them by His Spirit through the prophets (9.30). The writer of the Chronicles is the same (I Ch. 12.18, II Ch. 15.1-2, 18.12-27, 20.14, and 24.20). Also, Zechariah spoke of "the words which the Lord of hosts had sent by his Spirit through the former prophets" (7.12). Yet, undoubtedly the most important such statement from this period came from Joel (2.28-29):

> And it shall come to pass afterward, that I will pour out my spirit on all flesh; your sons and daughters shall prophesy, your old men shall dream dreams, and your young men shall see visions. [29]Even upon the menservants and the maidservants in those days, I will pour out my spirit.

Here Joel seems to have conflated the wish expressed by Moses in Nu. 11 and the outpouring of the spirit in Isaiah and Ezekiel, so that God would pour out his Holy Spirit indiscriminately on all groups of people with the result that they would be prophets.

To repeat the main point, in the OT the function of the Holy Spirit dwelling in a person was to provide that person with miraculous powers, especially prophecy. A very popular view current today with regard to the Holy Spirit is that it indwells persons, empowering them morally, that the indwelling presence of God gives people the ability to live a higher moral life, one higher than they would otherwise be able to attain. However, the evidence from the OT does not support this view of the Holy Spirit. In fact, there are many cases in the OT where the bearer of the Spirit did rather poorly morally. This is not to suggest that the indwelling of the Holy Spirit had a negative moral effect, but rather that it appears to have had no direct effect on the person at all. In fact, the prophet himself appeared to be just one more member of the audience of the prophetic word, and he might even find himself ignoring the message, like others around him.

There are several outstanding examples of this point. Jephthah had the Spirit, led the people of Israel to victory, but still practiced the pagan rite of child sacrifice (Ju. 11.29-40). Samson also disappoints us, despite God's continual working with him through the Spirit. Indeed, King Saul had the Spirit all through his early career as king, that is, until his jealousy overcame him. The point is that outstanding people had the indwelling Spirit in the OT, yet there is no indication of added moral benefit to them. The benefit of the Spirit came through inspired preaching. Passages like Ezk. 11.19-20 and 36.26-27 are often cited to the contrary, but, as we saw above, these passages are not really about the Holy Spirit after all.

There are some inferences we can draw from the presence of the Spirit, though. In the OT the presence of prophets or the lack thereof could signify the spiritual state of the people as a whole. There came a point in King Saul's life when God felt compelled to remove the Spirit from him. Even David feared the same fate at one point. The presence of the Spirit in the form of the column of smoke and the pillar of fire indicated God's protective presence with his people in the wilderness. In times of spiritual decline there was the threat that God would remove the Spirit from among them. However, upon their repentance at a later time God would quench their spiritual thirst by once again sending unto them prophets as one might pour water out on the parched desert floor.

The presence of the Spirit also appears to have served in a confirmatory way. The seventy appointed to assist Moses received the gift of prophecy. This gave them authority. Similarly with Joshua. Saul's gift of prophecy confirmed his selection as king, and his occasional fits of prophetic ecstasy indicated his error in pursuing David (I Sm. 19.8-24). Fulfilled prophecy served as a test between true and false prophets, and, as we stated above, the outpouring of the Spirit could be taken as a sign that God had renewed His relationship with His people.

We now turn to a survey of material not often studied in connection with the subject of the Holy Spirit, non-canonical Jewish writings and secular Graeco-Roman writings somewhat contemporaneous with the origin of the New Testament.

CHAPTER TWO

THE SPIRIT OF GOD IN JEWISH INTERTESTAMENTAL AND SECULAR GRAECO-ROMAN LITERATURE

It is generally known among more serious students of the Bible that there is a wealth of background material available for the one who wishes to get a better picture of the historical context out of which the NT came. Most of this material is Jewish. For example, there are the famous Dead Sea Scrolls, a collection of esoteric writings belonging to a group of Jewish monks during the first century A. D. and maybe two centuries before. There is also a rather large collection of apocryphal and apocalyptic writings from the same period. Then there is the very influential group of Jewish teachers known as the rabbis. They were responsible not only for some of the material mentioned already but also for a great amount of legal and ethical teachings later codified as the Talmud. The OT was also translated into other languages, such as Greek and Aramaic, with some interpretive additions occurring along the way. And finally, there are the writings of Josephus the historian and Philo the philosopher.

In this chapter I want to discuss some of the references to the Holy Spirit we find in the above material, but also in this chapter we shall take a brief look at some examples of how the Graeco-Roman world understood the divine spirit indwelling a human.

One of the main texts of the Dead Sea Scrolls is the manual of discipline, or the community rule, which stresses throughout the pure life, not only of the priests but of all the other members of the community as well. In chapters 3 and 4 we find the following discussion (all excerpts are taken from *The Dead Sea Scrolls in English*, tran. by Geza Vermes, 3rd ed., London: Penguin Books, 1962).

> He has created man to govern the world, and has appointed for him two spirits in which to walk until the time of His visitation: the spirits of truth and falsehood.
> ....
> All the children of righteousness are ruled by the Prince of Light and walk in the ways of light, but all the children of falsehood are ruled by the Angel of Darkness and walk in the ways of darkness.

The writer proceeds to list those virtues associated with the spirit of light and those vices associated with the spirit of darkness, after which he concludes with the following.

> The nature of all the children of men is ruled by these (two spirits), and during their life all the hosts of men have a portion of their divisions and walk in (both) their ways. And the whole reward for their deeds shall be, for everlasting ages, according to whether each man's portion in their two divisions is great or small. For God has established the spirits in equal measure until the final age, and has set everlasting hatred between their divisions. Truth abhors the works of falsehood, and falsehood hates all the ways of truth. And their struggle is fierce in all their arguments for they do not walk together.

This is not a passage about the Holy Spirit, but as we shall see later, it is important to an interpretation of certain NT passages. The two spirits in the excerpt above are not conscious entities; instead they are moral forces. However, there indeed do exist conscious entities which lead these forces, one the Prince of Light, the other the Angel of Darkness. These forces, or principles, dwell together in the hearts of all men, with men making their choices between them.

Though very often the Holy Spirit is mentioned in these scrolls in conjunction with prophecy, there is another unusual category of statements. In 1QH 7.6 (in The Thanksgiving Hymns) God is praised for shedding His Holy Spirit upon the worshiper, strengthening him so as to keep him from stumbling and purifying him from sin. Similarly, though man is merely a vessel of clay, God has chosen, at least for some, to shape a spirit (or in some cases spirits) which helps them to understand God's will. Now, this latter spirit is most likely not the Holy Spirit, since it is one which God has shaped. Moreover, as for *how* the Holy Spirit might strengthen, illuminate, and purify someone the Dead Sea Scrolls do not say, but given the intense devotion the communicants had to the Law of Moses, the most likely interpretation would be that the Spirit effected these spiritual changes upon human beings through the OT scriptures. On the other hand, it has been suggested that the writers might have been referring to themselves as prophets. It is known from history that they definitely believed such, so the references could be words of thanksgiving for God's gift of inspiration.

We now take up the works of the rabbis and enter the mainstream of Jewish thought in Jesus' day. In their apocalyptic writings we find some of the dualism we found in the Dead Sea Scrolls: there are two categories of spirits within man which influence him in one way or the other. However, when it comes to the Holy Spirit the function is clearly prophetic. Sometimes the terms "the Spirit of God" or "the Holy Spirit" are used, but the rabbis also began to use such terms as "a spirit of power," "a spirit of understanding," "the spirit of truth," "the spirit of prophecy," and even odd phrases, such as "the spirit of grace" *(The Testament of Judah* 24.3) interchangeably. These spirits are poured out, placed within, given to, and sent to various persons. They come upon, rest upon, descend upon, clothe, abide in, and speak through these persons as well. In nearly every case the results are visions, revelations, predictions, prophecies, scripture, and sometimes extraordinary powers (signs, wonders, miracles). For example, the spirit of power caused Enoch to "cry out" with a great voice, extolling God (I *Enoch* 71.11), a spirit of truth descended upon Rebecca's mouth, causing her to prophesy (*Jubilees* 25.14), and a spirit of prophecy came down upon Jacob's mouth (*Jubilees* 31.12).

Similarly, when we come to the legal and ethical traditions of the rabbis, as they are found in the Talmud, we find pretty much the same thing: the Holy Spirit functions primarily as the giver of the faculty of prophecy. This can be seen in some representative examples like the following. In Genesis Rabbah 37.7 on 10.5 Rabbi Simon ben Gamliel explains, "The ancients, because they could avail themselves of the Holy Spirit, named themselves in reference to [forthcoming] events; but we who cannot avail themselves of the Holy Spirit are named after our fathers" (My quotations are from the translations by H. Freeman and Maurice Simon, *The Midrash Rabbah*, London: The Soncino Press, 5 vols., 1977, and *The Babylonian Talmud*, ed. by Isidore Epstein, 18 vols., London: The Soncino Press, 1940). Or, as in Genesis Rabbah 93:12 on 45:14, Rabbi Eleazar says, "In fact, he foresaw through the Holy Spirit that two temples would be built in Benjamin's portion, and both would be destroyed." And many more such examples could be given.

In the Talmud we find the same ethical dualism as has been discussed already however without reference to spirits of any sort. For the rabbis there are two forces at work in each adult, the Good Impulse and the Evil Impulse. Most of what was said above would apply to these two impulses.

The rabbis added some aspects to the understanding of the Holy Spirit current in their day. For example, there was much discussion about why the Holy Spirit departed a people. They concluded that it had departed the Gentiles after Balaam's misuse of his gift and had departed the Jews after the destruction of the first temple. After that time for the Jews there were only rare occurrences of God's voice being heard, a function of the Holy Spirit, but rare and only for the most deserving.

The removal of the Holy Spirit from the Jews was an application of the principle that righteousness was a prerequisite for the Holy Spirit to dwell and among them. Nowhere in the rabbinic literature does the Holy Spirit generate personal righteousness, instead the dispensation of the Holy Spirit was regarded as a reward for especially great holiness. Neither was possession of the Holy Spirit requisite for one to understand scripture, but quite the reverse. In 'Abodah Zara 20 B, Rabbi Phineas ben Jair is quoted: "Study leads to precision, precision leads to zeal, zeal leads to meekness, meekness leads to fear of sin, fear of sin leads to saintliness, saintliness leads to the [possession of] the holy spirit, the holy spirit leads to life eternal, and saintliness is greater than any of these, ..." In fact, whereas the Holy Spirit had been taken away from Israel because of their sin, the rabbis taught that when the people had repented sincerely enough the Messiah would come and bestow the Holy Spirit on all of Israel so that they all would be prophets, just as Moses had wished.

In the rabbis also we find that for a people to have the Holy Spirit it was not necessary that they each had the indwelling Spirit, but rather only that there were some among them who were prophets.

The rabbis also discussed at great length how there are measures of Spirit possession. Just as some of Moses' spirit was taken from him and placed on the seventy elders without Moses' measure being diminished at all, different persons of great note among the Jews had had different measures of the Spirit. In Leviticus Rabbah 15.2 on 13.2, Rabbi Aha says, "Even the Holy Spirit resting on the prophets does so by weight, one prophet speaking one book of prophecy and another speaking two books."

The rabbis, living at a time when the Jews had become a people of The Book, also began to identify the Holy Spirit with scripture, and vice versa. For one to read a passage of scripture is indeed to have the Holy Spirit talking to him directly. Furthermore, in one place a rabbi might respond, "The Law says such and such," and in another place and just as easily say, "The Holy Spirit says such and such."

Lastly, it is thought by some that the term "the Holy Spirit" itself was a rabbinic invention. It is true that anything like that term is rare, or even nonexistent, before the time of the rabbis, so perhaps to them do the NT writers owe their use of the term.

As we noted at the first of this chapter, the OT had been translated into other languages at the time of Jesus and the apostles. One of the languages was Greek, and the translation is known as the Septuagint. Nothing really significantly different occurs in most of the Holy Spirit passages except for a few apparent anomalies, like this passage in Wisdom 9.13-18.

> [13]For what man can learn the counsel of God?
> Or who can discern what the Lord wills?
>
> [14]For the reasoning of mortals is worthless,
> and our designs are likely to fail,
>
> [15]for a perishable body weighs down the soul,
> and this earthly tent burdens the thoughtful mind.
>
> [16]We can hardly guess at what is on earth,
> what is at hand we find with labor;
> but who has traced out what is in the heavens?

> ¹⁷Who has learned thy counsel, unless thou hast given wisdom
> and sent thy holy Spirit from on high?
> ¹⁸And thus the paths of those on earth were set right,
> and men were taught what pleases thee,
> and were saved by wisdom.

Some interpreters see something very different here, that the Jewish notion of spirit has been transformed. This passage as been singled out as an example of a burgeoning new viewpoint of the Holy Spirit as the essential source of moral and religious life. However, such is not the case; no transformation has occurred at all. The subject of this text is Solomon's wisdom, and Solomon's wisdom in the Jewish mind was the epitome of inspiration. Similarly, the passage above simply acknowledges that without special revelation, man by reason alone, would never be able to discern the will of God very clearly. Once again, the possession of the Spirit in this passage carries prophetic powers.

A more interesting translation of the OT was that known as the Targums. After the destruction of the temple in the sixth century B.C.E., study of the Torah became increasingly prominent in the lives of the Jews. The synagogue served this purpose especially. Because of exile and dispersion many Jews spoke Aramaic instead of Hebrew, so the Torah was often studied in its translated form (targum). Actually, targums were more than translations; interpretative changes and additions abound in them. Some of these changes have to do with dogma, others have to do with reverential language about God, and others were obviously intended to render the passage clearer in meaning.

One aspect of targummic interpretation which is relevant to our concerns is the general tendency in the Targums toward the transcendentalization of God. For example, anthropomorphisms, such as "God's hand," are replaced by literal expressions, such as "inspiration." Expressions about God's repentance are changed. God's infinite attributes are emphasized, where the Hebrew text brings God more down to earth. In other words, God is kept away from human beings at the greatest distance possible. A few examples will suffice.

The Targum on Gn. 41.38 has Pharoah asking, "Can we find a man like this in whom there is the spirit of prophecy?" The Hebrew text has "the Spirit of the Lord," but the targummic writer could not countenance a human being having in him the very Holy Spirit. So they changed the expression to "the spirit of prophecy ." This is very instructive to us in that we can see how the Holy Spirit was understood at this time, namely, as that entity which bestowed miraculous powers, especially prophecy. In fact, throughout the Aramaic Bible the translators were thoroughly consistent in seeing the Spirit as prophetic and in never placing the Spirit itself in human beings.

So, when we look at the Targums on Ezk. 11.19 and 36.26-7, passages which we noted in Chapter One, we find that God is said to have put within the people a faithful spirit, except in the last verse, where it says, "And My holy spirit will I put deep inside of you . . . ." (The English translation is by Samuel H. Levy, in *The Aramaic Bible*, ed. by Martin McNamara, Wilmington, Del.: Michael Glazier, Inc., 1988.) That could mean only that for the Aramaic translators Ezekiel is not talking about the Holy Spirit, but a holy spirit instead.

One last example from the Targums might be given here, not as a passage on the Holy Spirit but rather as an example of an interesting interpretation which we shall have cause to mention again. The Targum on Gn. 2.7 (in all three basic sources) reads as follows: "Now the Lord God created Adam as dust from the earth and breathed into (the nostrils of) his face the breath of life and it became in Adam a spirit uttering speech." The translator here interpreted "living being" as a spirit uttering speech, thus emphasizing man's faculty of speech as his preeminence over beasts.

When we summarize the data from the Targums we once again find in the Jewish background of Jesus' day an understanding of the Holy Spirit which is simple and uniform; the indwelling Holy Spirit provides miraculous power (especially prophecy) and that alone.

Philo Judaeus lived from 30 B.C.E. to 40 C.E. This Alexandrian Jew represented an equal blend of Judaism and Hellenism, a blend which is quite evident in his allegories of OT stories. He even went so far as to identify one sense of "the spirit of God" with physical air in the prescientific sense current in his day, though that meaning was not very important to him. Another sense of "the spirit of God" was that divine spark in man which urges him to focus on the highest things, but the spirit of God in this sense, according to Philo, cannot abide in man but temporarily; every man has fleeting encounters with higher things, but in general they are only fleeting.

In the main, Philo saw the indwelling Holy Spirit as prophetic. God's Spirit upon Moses and the seventy enabled them to excel over the other Israelites, yet even this sense of the Spirit could not be said to abide in men indefinitely because of the flesh. Only those who would abandon worldly concerns and truly humble themselves before God could enjoy the divine spirit of wisdom abiding upon them for a long time. Such was the case with Moses. He became even more than the seventy; he became a revealer of divine rites. So evidently, Philo meant that Moses enjoyed divine revelation, for he grouped Moses among the sages and prophets.

One of the most interesting passages on the role of the Spirit in inspiration can be found in his work *On Special Laws* 3.48:

> For no pronouncement of a Prophet is ever his own; he is an interpreter prompted by Another in all his utterances, when knowing not what he does he is filled with inspiration, as the reason withdraws and surrenders the citadel of the soul to a new visitor and tenant, the Divine Spirit which plays upon the vocal organism and dictates words which so clearly express its prophetic message.

Clearly, the Holy Spirit here inspires prophecy for Philo, and in doing so it overwhelms the prophet. The prophetic message is not merely the brightest ideas of the human mind but rather the direct product of the indwelling Spirit.

Philo was also much like the rabbis in that he thought that great moral righteousness sometimes merited the reception of God's Spirit and not that God's Spirit caused one to be righteous. In fact, Philo thought that not often does one even attain such a degree of righteousness.

Flavius Josephus is our last Jewish author. Josephus was a Jewish general in the tragic war against the Romans during 66-70 C.E. He survived to write a history of the war and of the Jewish people and is a primary source of our knowledge of this period, including information about Jesus, John the Baptizer, and James the brother of Jesus. However, besides using the phrase "the divine spirit" he offers nothing new to our understanding of the background; for him the divine spirit is God's Spirit inspiring prophecy.

So, the material from Jewish intertestamental literature speaks with one voice with regard to the Holy Spirit. God's Spirit indwelling a human being empowers that human to do miraculous things, especially to prophesy.

But before we go to the NT let us look briefly at some secular literature of the time; after all, the language of the Greek world played a large part in the background of the NT, it being the language of the original texts. Moreover, Luke was probably not a Jew, but rather a Gentile polished by the literature of Greece and Rome. The culture of the Roman Empire affected all the subcultures in the Empire, including Palestine's, so due attention should be given to this category of data as well.

Even though the Greek word for spirit can as well mean breath, wind, ghost, and many similar concepts, we find in the earliest Greek period much more commonly the older and related term for breath. When we find that term in association with a deity, it actually refers to a god's breath. However, its use was metaphorical. A god influenced some person by breathing upon him, thus inspiring him. For example, Homer in *The Odyssey* has Penelope ascribing her plan to weave the robe to some "god breathed" thought (19.138-40). Similarly, the Muses inspired artists by breathing upon them. Military generals, like Lycurgus and Scipio, convinced their soldiers that they were guided by divine breath.

By the time Aeschylus wrote his plays (500 B.C.E), the term for spirit which we find in the NT had come into use among the Greeks as the common term for the divine breath. By far the most common association is the miraculous, especially the prophetic. Possessors of the divine breath had superhuman powers and could speak in such ways as to reflect inspiration, especially in the posture of foretellers.

However, for the Greeks the concept of divine inspiration was far more ecstatic than we find in the rabbis. This is especially evident in the many discussions of the Delphic oracle. In Delphi, at the base of Mount Parnassos, where Apollo the god of prophecy dwelt, there was a cavern out of which occasionally blew a draft, which came to be regarded as Apollo's breath. Early on, a sheep had been caught in this draft and became wildly berserk. Later, a cult of prophetesses, the Sibyls, lived there, and upon being cajoled to ascend a tripod situated in the cavern they would become inspired with revelations about the ones who had come seeking their oracles. The futures of such seekers were not only foretold but told in rhythmic verse. Vergil tells of Aeneas seeking the Sibyline oracle *(The Aeneid,* 6.9-12, 42-51, in *Virgil,* trans. by H. Rushton Fairclough, *Loeb Classical Library,* 2 vols., rev. ed., 1918, I., pp. 506-11).

> But good Aeneas seeks the heights, where Apollo
> sits enthroned, and a vast cavern hard by,
> hidden haunt of the dread Sibyl, into whom
> the Delian seer breathes a mighty mind and soul,
> revealing the future.
> . . . .
> The huge side of the Euboean rock is hewn into
> a cavern, whither lead a hundred wide mouths,
> a hundred gateways, whence rush as many
> voices, the answers of the Sibyl. They had come
> to the threshold, when the maiden cries, "Tis time
> to ask the oracles; the god, lo! the god!" As
> thus she spake before the doors, suddenly
> nor countenance nor color was the same, nor
> stayed her tresses braided; but her bosom
> heaves, her heart swells with wild frenzy, and she
> is taller to behold, nor has her voice a mortal
> ring since now she feels the nearer breath of deity.

From this account we can see the mainly emotional and anti-noetic character of the Greek inspiration. Plutarch later wrote a great deal about this phenomenon, which had ceased by his day (100 C.E.), which state of affairs he referred to as "the quenching of the spirit."

We also find in Graeco-Roman literature two accounts of miraculous births associated with the divine breath. In Aeschylus, Epaphras became the father of a race when his mother Io, a priestess, was impregnated by the divine breath of Zeus. Later, Plutarch argued that since the divine spirit had on occasion had intercourse with women, it would follow that the same spirit would also visit great leaders and prophets to inspire them.

A peculiarly Greek notion of spirit is the materialistic view of it as moving air. However, it is not completely physical; it has a certain eternal quality to it, and for the Stoics it served as the basic constituent of all things, both living and non-living. The Stoics then went on to fix the essence of God as an intelligent and fiery air which pervades the universe.

Finally, as we saw in Philo, the Greeks sometimes spoke of the divine spirit as that rational part of all human beings which lifted them above brute beasts. However, there is no emphasis placed on this spirit as providing any moral empowerment.

So, the secular literature, very much like the other we have perused, has it that the spirit of a god, when visited upon a human being, endows that human with extraordinary power, especially that of prophetic utterance.

CHAPTER THREE

THE HOLY SPIRIT IN MATTHEW AND MARK

We have now come to the focus of this whole work, the analysis of the Holy Spirit as presented in the NT. All of the data surveyed so far serve as background to our understanding of the NT documents. These documents were born in a world which already knew the OT, the intertestamental literature of Palestinian Judaism, and the much respected Greek and Roman literature. Surely the writers of the NT were responsible to communicate their new teachings in terms which they knew would be understood by their readers in certain ways. In fact, the categories of meaning established in the preceding chapters should be given priority as candidate interpretations as we come to the various relevant NT passages. New interpretations should require special justification before being accepted.

As we come to the NT we will find many passages which clearly refer to the human spirit, to breath, wind, to evil spirits, etc. If it is obvious that these are the referents, then these passages will be ignored. Our concern shall be to understand those passages which speak of the Spirit of God, especially as it is found indwelling human beings.

In this chapter we shall look at Matthew and Mark. Wherever these two writers coincide we will study them together. Luke, himself the writer of two documents, Luke and Acts, will be treated separately in the next chapter, since he is the major contributor to the NT; though on occasion we will compare Luke's version of the gospel with Matthew's and Mark's. Later we will look at the combined writings attributed to John, the writings of Paul, and the rest of the NT.

Our first NT encounter with the Holy Spirit is in the birth narrative of Jesus (Mt. 1.18-20). There we find Mary miraculously pregnant with Jesus by the Holy Spirit. The term "the Holy Spirit," which was so rare in the OT, is employed by the Gospel writers without any explanation, indicating the influence of the rabbis during this period. As we saw in the last chapter, there are examples in Greek literature of gods mingling with humans, resulting in the births of very special people. We find the same thing here, a miraculous conception and the birth of a very special person. It is possible therefore to think of God as using an existent category, namely that of divine births, to make a point about Jesus, the point being that Jesus was destined to be a eminent person, and in this case the most eminent person ever.

Next we find John the Baptizer deferring to Jesus as the one who would baptize people with the Holy Spirit and fire (Mt. 3.11-12), probably the most significant passage from our two writers on the work of the Spirit.

> I baptize you with water for repentance, but he who is coming after me is mightier than I, whose sandals I am not worthy to carry; he will baptize you with the Holy Spirit and with fire. [12]His winnowing fork is in his hand, and he will clear his threshing floor and gather his wheat into the granary, but the chaff he will burn with unquenchable fire.

However, in Mark's account (1.7-8) instead of a baptism of the Spirit and of fire it is said only that Jesus "will baptize you with the Holy Spirit." So, several questions immediately spring up. Are there two baptisms, one of the Holy Spirit and one of fire? Why is there no fire in Mark's account? And what is the relationship between Holy Spirit baptism, fire baptism, and water baptism? There are four classic sets of answers to these three questions, plus one recent one, which we will consider below.

(1) Chrysotom (400 C.E.) related the fire to the Holy Spirit. In favor of this view is the appearance of the tongues of fire on Pentecost (Ac. 2). However, this view has generally been abandoned for two reasons. The judgment aspect, eminent in the burning of the chaff (Mt. 3.12), is too obvious to ignore. In the OT this imagery is always negative, reflecting God's judgment upon sinners and His separating the righteous from the unrighteous via an invading army (cf. Is. 17.4-6, 21.10, 41.15-16, Je. 51.33, Joel 3.13; cf. Mt. 13.30). So, if the fire had reference to the Holy Spirit, it becomes difficult to understand where the judgment imagery might fit in. Furthermore, there is no clear corroboration of the association of fire with the Spirit in any other NT passages.

(2) Origen (200 C.E.) took the passages to speak of two baptisms: of those who repented with the Holy Spirit, and of the unrepentant with the fire of punishment. The passages speak of the wheat in the granary, so the Holy Spirit must be a blessing. Also, the Dead Sea Scrolls speak of the Holy Spirit as a gracious blessing. But the baptism of fire is a punishment, so there must be two baptisms here. The objections to this view are mainly grammatical and will be examined below.

(3) Some have argued that the original form of the passage omitted "the Holy Spirit" and that it was only a judgment statement. Evidently, an Aramaic reconstruction of the passage can be made to support this view, but against this interpretation is the lack of any other mention of the baptism of fire. Furthermore, there is Mark's mention of the Holy Spirit but omission of fire in the parallel passage (Mk. 1.8). So, clearly in this episode there was mention of a baptism of the Spirit.

(4) Surprisingly, many commentators have taken the Baptizer's statement to refer to a divine fiery wind of judgment with no reference to the Holy Spirit. As we have already stated, the word for spirit can also be translated "wind," but this interpretation disregards the merciful side of the statement. Even more telling is the fact that this baptism is not presented as a threat. The recipients of John's baptism are not threatened with messianic baptism as a fearful alternative, nor is John's baptism a way of escape from the coming one's baptism.

(5) This last interpretation, a recent one, holds that the early church synthesized the various types of baptism by making water baptism a symbol of baptism in the Holy Spirit (cf. I Co. 12.13). According to this view, Paul put together the judgment and mercy by emphasizing water baptism as a baptism into Christ's death (cf. Ro. 6.1ff), wherein is found both grace and death.

The problem with this last interpretation is that it has John the Baptizer needlessly coining a new term. There is a very likely candidate for the background of Mt 3.11-12, namely, Joel 2.28-29, where we have an outpouring of both the Spirit and judgment. Furthermore, this view has John identifying water baptism with Holy Spirit baptism, which is exactly what John is contrasting. John himself baptizes with water; the Messiah would have another baptism.

View (2) is the most plausible. The main objection against it has been grammatical. It has been stated that since John said, "He will baptize you with the Holy Spirit and fire," the "you" indicates that they all would receive the same thing, and the "with," being an unrepeated preposition (in the Greek), ties the two aspects together. But such is not the case, as only one of many examples will show. In Mt. 10.18 we find, "You will be dragged before governors and kings . . . ." Here Jesus warns his disciples that some of them, in various combinations, will stand before governors on some occasions, and that others of them will stand before kings on other occasions. Similarly, there is no grammatical reason in Mt. 3.11-12 why John could not have meant that Jesus was bringing two new baptisms, not associated with water, one of the Holy Spirit and one of fire, each of which will be experienced by only one of two distinct groups of people. However, it still remains to be seen what these two baptisms are, a question which will not be addressed until the chapter on Luke.

Our next passage is the account of Jesus' baptism in water by John where John protested by saying that he should be baptized by Jesus instead (Mt.3.13-17, Mk. 1.9-11). Even though Jesus did baptize people in water (Jn. 4.1ff.), in light of the previous discussion John should probably be understood as requesting the baptism of the Holy Spirit. Jesus, of course, insisted on being immersed in water by John.

Though the Holy Spirit appears on this occasion in the form of a bird, the only thing which is significant about it is that it served as a confirmation of Jesus' special role (cf. Jn. 1.29-34). (If we also compare Luke's version, 3.21-22, we find that the terms "the Spirit of God," "the Spirit," and "the Holy Spirit" can be interchangeable.) This is also the time which marks the coming of the Spirit upon Jesus. There is no indication that Jesus had the Spirit in the womb, as did his kinsman John (Lk. 1.15), and neither is there any indication that Jesus had the Spirit before his baptism. Jesus' first miracle, in fact, was performed in Cana shortly after he began his ministry as a man of thirty (Jn. 2.11, Lk. 3.23). In a summary sort of way, Peter described "how God anointed Jesus of Nazareth with the Holy Spirit and with power; how he went about doing good and healing all that were oppressed by the devil, for God was with him" (Ac. 10.38). Finally, Luke, who reflects a much greater interest in the work of the Holy Spirit than do any of the other NT writers, explicitly says that Jesus returned from the Jordan "full of the Spirit" (4.1). So if, as is often suggested, Jesus received the Holy Spirit at his baptism, and as it is also taught, that Jesus never sinned (He. 4.15), his sinless perfection cannot be attributed to the indwelling of the Holy Spirit.

Jesus' reception of the Spirit constituted his empowerment as a miracle worker and a prophet. As we see, immediately after Jesus' baptism the Spirit drives Jesus into the wilderness to be tempted of the devil (Mt. 4.1-2, Mk. 1.12-13). Jesus is thus depicted as a prophet very much like Ezekiel and Elijah, personally directed in his prophetic mission by the Holy Spirit. Mark, especially, seems to portray the Spirit as directing Jesus into the insecurity of the wilderness, where he had to live with wild beasts and be alone to confront the devil, after which Jesus can begin to despoil the devil's kingdom by casting demons out of those possessed.

This is one of the few passages in the Bible about being led by the Spirit. It is an issue more on the minds of modern Christians than on the minds of the earliest ones. Jesus' being led by the Spirit should not be considered a model for us today. There is nothing about an inward leading here. Moreover, Jesus was led into a very strenuous situation, one of pain and trial, hardly the kind of thing which might be used to offer comfort to someone. If this episode is a model for us today, it provides us with a frightful prospect.

Moving on to Mk. 2.8, it says, "And immediately Jesus perceiving in his spirit that they thus questioned within themselves, said to them, 'Why do you question thus in your heart?'" This makes no reference to the Holy Spirit. In the parallel verse in Matthew it just says that Jesus knew their thoughts (cf. Mk. 8.11-12). Similarly, when Jesus died and gave up his spirit (Mt. 27.50, Mk. 15.37), it was his human spirit.

Later in Mt. 10.17-20 Jesus promised his disciples that at a later hour they would be persecuted but also that "the spirit of your Father" would speak through them, so that they need not even prepare their remarks. This is obviously a reference to prophecy. (Cf. Mt. 24.19-20, Mk. 13.11.)

A most interesting story is that of the accusation that Jesus was casting out demons by the power of Satan (Mt. 12.28-32, Mk. 3.27-30). Despite the complexities of Jesus' response to the charges of his enemies, the underlying principle is that "a tree is known by its fruits;" so, if a person casts out demons he cannot be of Satan, but rather of God. In fact, it would have to have been clear to them that they had just seen a miracle inspired by the Holy Spirit. Based on this underlying premise, Jesus concluded that their animosity toward him had closed their minds to the most obvious truth. Their own stubbornness had driven them to assign the miracles of the Holy Spirit to Satan. Jesus allowed for them to blaspheme him. After all, from all appearances, he was just another man. It was the miracles that made him different, and they were not up for debate. In fact, not even the Pharisees denied that he worked miracles which resulted in great good in the lives of human beings. Thus their ascription of these miracles to the power of Satan was blatant blasphemy.

Jesus continued by saying that such blasphemy is unforgivable. Much theologizing can enter here, but the most plausible explanation is that people who would reject even miracles are so impenetrable that God will never be able to get through to them. It is possible that Jesus was cautioning the Pharisees about just how close they had gotten to that impenetrable point. At any rate, Mark stated that it was because the Pharisees had said that Jesus had an unclean spirit that Jesus warned them about the unforgivable status of blasphemy against the Holy Spirit. There is no doubt from this passage that the Holy Spirit is very closely associated with Jesus' miracle-working power, so that the sin of blasphemy against the Holy Spirit can be said to occur when one ascribes to Satan miracles which in reality come from the Spirit.

Bible readers over the years have often experienced alarm at this passage. The very mention of an unforgivable sin raises fears that one might have committed it. However, I would suggest that, as we have seen, the aspect of the miracles is quite relevant here. If one were to reject miracles, or, which is tantamount to rejection, ascribe them to Satan, then he too might be guilty of an unforgivable sin, or at least approach such. Moreover, one might be said to commit such a sin today if he were to assume a similar posture of close-minded defiance (cf. I Jn. 5.16-17).

These are the major passages on the Spirit from Matthew and Mark, but some minor ones would include Mt. 22.43 and Mk. 12.36, where Jesus refers to the Psalms as the work of David in the Spirit, a reference to the work of the Spirit in inspiration. And finally, we have one of the few putative Trinitarian statements, The Great Commission, where Jesus commands his disciples to make more disciples by baptizing people in the name of the Father, and the Son, and the Holy Spirit (Mt. 28.18-20). We will take a brief look at the issue of the Trinity in the last chapter.

This concludes our study of Matthew and Mark; and even though their statements about the Holy Spirit are sketchy, there are several points which can be made. First, "the Holy Spirit" is fairly common and is consistently represented as indwelling persons (John and Jesus) and inspiring them with miracle-working powers, especially prophecy (John the Baptizer never worked a miracle). The presentation of Matthew and Mark is very similar to that of the rabbis, leaving us with the conclusion that the latter had had a great influence upon the writing styles of the former. We found no attempt on their part to introduce any new concept of the Spirit.

We also saw how John the baptizer introduced the baptism of the Holy Spirit but from the very beginning distinguished it sharply from water baptism. John eagerly anticipated the baptism of the Holy Spirit as a blessing from God upon the penitent but dreaded the coming judgmental baptism of fire. Neither Matthew nor Mark clarified the natures of these two latter forms of baptism, but it was clear that repentance and/or conversion (through water baptism) prepared the recipients for the baptism of the Holy Spirit, while resistance to John's call to repentance preceded the baptism of fire.

Our examination of blasphemy against the Holy Spirit also drew a connection between the Spirit and miracles. It was because the miracles were so obvious that that such blasphemy was so serious. It is therefore highly questionable whether the sin of blasphemy against the Holy Spirit could even occur without the presence of miracles.

We should also note that nowhere in these two gospels do we find Jesus making any connection between the Holy Spirit and either ethical behavior or practical abilities concerning living a righteous life, not even in his own life. This is remarkable. In fact, if the Spirit were associated with moral improvement and if the Spirit were a special element in the coming age, then Jesus' moral criticisms, such as those of the Pharisees, would seem to be inappropriate and unjustified. Rather, one's moral improvement appears to have been a precondition for the reception of the baptism of the Holy Spirit.

Matthew's and Mark's gospels do not really tell us a great deal about the Holy Spirit with respect to conversion;

neither do they tell us much about baptism in the Holy Spirit. The most informative writer on these matters would be Luke, in his gospel but especially in the Book of Acts. So, to the writings of Luke we now turn.

CHAPTER FOUR

THE HOLY SPIRIT IN LUKE AND ACTS

Luke is by far the clearest of all the NT writers about the Holy Spirit. The Spirit is a major character in his treatises, and the work of the Spirit is a major theme in his story line. Though we start with his gospel, many issues have already been covered by our exposition of the parallel accounts in Matthew and Mark. The Book of Acts, however, will require very special attention.

Much of the narrative of Jesus' birth is found only in Luke. Not only does he tell of the miraculous impregnation of Mary by the Spirit, but there are all the attendant stories of persons being filled with the Holy Spirit and prophesying with regard to the Christ child. Elizabeth, for example, is told that she will give birth to a baby who would have the Holy Spirit from birth and would one day prepare the people for the coming of the Lord (Lk. 1.15-17). Again in Lk. 1, upon becoming pregnant, Mary went to her kinswoman Elizabeth.

> [41]And when Elizabeth heard the greeting of Mary, the babe leaped in her womb; and Elizabeth was filled with the Holy Spirit and she exclaimed with a loud voice,[42]"Blessed are you among women, and blessed is the fruit of your womb. [43]And why is this granted me, that the mother of my Lord should come to me?"

Very much like some of the examples in the apocalyptic writings of the rabbis, we find the Holy Spirit coming upon someone, empowering that person with the ability to prophesy. Later, Zechariah, husband of Elizabeth, was also "filled with the Holy Spirit and prophesied" that John would be a great prophet (Lk. 1.67-80). Ana prophesied (2.36-38), but there was no explicit mention of the Holy Spirit. And finally there was Simeon (2.25-35);

> and this man was righteous and devout, looking for the consolation of Israel, [26]and the Holy Spirit was upon him. And it had been revealed to him by the Holy Spirit that he would not see death before he had seen the Lord's Christ. [27]And inspired by the Spirit he came into the temple; and when the parents brought in the child Jesus, to do for him according to the custom of the law, [28]he took him up in his arms and blessed God and said,[29]"Lord, now lettest thou thy servant depart in peace according to thy word; [30]for mine eyes have seen thy salvation [31]which thou hast prepared in the presence of all peoples, [32]a light for revelation to the Gentiles, and for glory to thy people Israel."

These early passages set the tone for Luke, the NT writer who mentions the Holy Spirit more than any other. For Luke, for one to have the Holy Spirit means that he has the prophetic faculty. In fact, it has been argued by some that for Luke the Holy Spirit means only prophecy, not even miracles of any other nature, not moral empowerment, not anything but prophecy. If so, this would explain a rather strange phenomenon we find in Lk. 11.20-23, the story of the Pharisees' charge that Jesus was casting out demons by the power of Satan. As we saw in the last chapter, Matthew, who was very Jewish in his orientation, has Jesus argue in the following manner, "But if it is by the Spirit of God that I cast out demons, then the kingdom of God has come upon you" (12.28). But Luke has, "But if it is by the finger of God that I cast out demons, then the kingdom of God has come upon you." Now the phrase "finger of God" comes right out of the OT. One would expect that of Matthew; and since Luke emphasizes the Holy Spirit so much, one would have expected him to mention it here also, but not so. The solution to this puzzle is that for Luke casting out demons is not the work of the Holy Spirit; only prophecy is.

We now come to a central passage, Lk. 24.44-53 and Ac. 1.1-2.47. It starts out with the post-resurrection Jesus interpreting the OT to his small group of disciples, showing them how in the OT one can find the death, burial, and resurrection of the Messiah. He then reminded them that they were witnesses to these things, a fact to which Luke would return several times, and then, on the basis of their role as witnesses, Jesus stated, "And behold, I send the promise of my Father upon you; but stay in the city until you are clothed with power from on high" (Lk. 24.48-49).

The Book of Acts takes up immediately where Luke's gospel leaves off, the post-resurrection appearances. "And while staying with them he charged them not to depart from Jerusalem, but to wait for the promise of the Father, which, he said, 'you heard from me, for John baptized with water, but before many days you shall be baptized with the Holy Spirit'" (Ac. 1.4-5). Again Jesus said, "But you shall receive power when the Holy Spirit has come upon you; and you shall be my witnesses in Jerusalem and in all Judea and Samaria and to the end of the earth" (Ac. 1.8).

Several important points can be established already. Since the disciples had this role as witnesses, they were to wait in the city of Jerusalem for the Father's promise, a promise which involved their being clothed with power from on high. This promise, this being clothed with power, was also referred to as the baptism of the Holy Spirit.

After witnessing Jesus going up into the clouds, the disciples returned to Jerusalem, where they devoted themselves to prayer along with the other disciples. During this time they chose Matthias to fill the spot vacated by

Judas, so that he could join the eleven as a witness to the resurrection of Jesus.

Then,

> ¹when the day of Pentecost had come, they were altogether in one place. ²And suddenly a sound came from heaven like the rush of a mighty wind, and it filled all the house where they were sitting. ³And there appeared to them tongues as of fire, distributed and resting on each one of them. ⁴And they were all filled with the Holy Spirit and began to speak in other tongues, as the Spirit gave them utterance (Ac. 2.1-4).

The wind is part of the evidence that the Spirit had come upon them. "Wind" is another possible translation for the word "spirit," and is often used metaphorically for the spirit. Fire also was associated with the Holy Spirit in Jewish background literature.

This event is the fulfillment of the promise Jesus gave them concerning the baptism of the Holy Spirit, the promise of the Father, which would clothe them with power so that they could be witnesses. The first actual effect was that the disciples began to speak in foreign languages, fourteen of which are actually listed in the text, and what the visiting foreigners heard was the disciples glorifying God for His mighty acts. I will suggest later that tongue-speaking was not practiced for teaching and preaching, but only for praising God, as appears to be the case here in this passage (2.12).

When Peter was able to get the crowd's attention and address their concerns, he began by asserting that this very thing which the people had witnessed that day was the fulfillment of Joel's prophecy (Joel 2.28-32), which we discussed in Chapter One. However, there are three places where Peter's quotation of Joel differs from both the Hebrew OT and the Septuagint (the Greek OT). In the latter two texts vs. 17 simply states that said events would take place by and by, but Luke has Peter saying that they would occur in the last days. This adds a distinctive apocalyptic character to the Pentecost events. The second addition is the reiteration of "prophecy" in vs. 18. Peter was probably recalling the emphasis laid on prophecy by the rabbis as a special indication of the coming of the messianic age. The third addition makes a distinction between wonders both in the heavens and upon the earth, whereas the wonders originally had to do with the celestial cataclysms listed in vv. 19 and 20. It has been suggested that the additions of "above" and "signs below" allow Peter to refer to the aforementioned prophecy as a sign. At any rate, all three of these changes have to do with making Joel's prophecy refer to the events of Pentecost as confirmatory manifestations of the impending messianic age.

Indeed, the thrust of the whole sermon was that there was plenty of proof that Jesus was truly raised from the dead, thus confirming his claims to be the Messiah. Peter mentioned Jesus' miracles, and he quoted the Psalms to that effect. Then he added,

> [32]This Jesus God raised up, and of that we are all witnesses. [33]Being therefore exalted at the right hand of God, and having received from the Father the promise of the Holy Spirit, he has poured out this which you see and hear.

Once again, we find the all-important witness theme with Peter laying claim to the role as witness to the resurrection of Jesus. But why should the people believe him? The answer to that question was right before them, what they were seeing and hearing, the tongues of fire, the rush of a mighty wind, and the miraculous tongue-speaking. Therefore, on the basis of the miraculous events of that day the Pentecost observers could know with certainty that Jesus was both Lord and Christ (vs. 36).

> [37] Now when they heard this they were cut to the heart, and said to Peter and the rest of the apostles, "Brethren, what shall we do?" [38] And Peter said to them, "Repent, and be baptized every one of you in the name of Jesus Christ for the remission of your sins; and you shall receive the gift of the Holy Spirit. [39] For the promise is to you and to your children and to all that are far off, everyone whom the Lord our God calls to him."

The manifestations of the Holy Spirit had their proper impact. People's minds were changed, and they felt the pain for what they had done to Jesus. They then asked the natural question, "What shall we do?" Upon the basis of their new faith, they were told, they should repent and be baptized in the name of the Messiah, so that their sins might be forgiven. Both repentance and baptism were put forth as conditions of their salvation. Repentance is basically a commitment to turn away from wrongdoing and to turn toward righteousness. But what is this baptism in the name of Jesus Christ? Since the baptism of the Holy Spirit was a promise, for which even Jesus' apostles had to wait, baptism in Jesus' name would appear to be something else, a command to be obeyed without hesitation. Also, upon being baptized and receiving the forgiveness of sins, they would receive further the gift of the Holy Spirit. So, baptism in Jesus' name and the baptism of the Holy Spirit are two different things, as will be made eminently clear when we examine the latter half of Ac. 8.

So then, what is this gift of the Holy Spirit? In Ac. 10 it will become clear that the baptism of the Holy Spirit, receiving the Holy Spirit, receiving the *gift* of the Holy Spirit, and having the Holy Spirit fall upon a person are all the same thing. Peter was therefore promising them that they too would receive, upon their being saved, the indwelling Holy Spirit, resulting in the ability to prophesy, see visions, and receive revelations. For, he says, the promise is not only for those who were there that day, but also to their children, to those far off (i.e., Gentiles; cf. Ep. 2.11-13), and all those whom Jesus would call.

One should be careful at this point. Peter's assurance to their children does not necessarily imply perpetuity. Joel's prophecy explicitly said "to your sons and daughters." Would that mean also that the gifts were for their children's children and their children's children's children? Not necessarily. Peter was probably saying only that the baptism of the Holy Spirit would be of wide distribution (as the prophecy states). This wide distribution of the outpouring of the Holy Spirit would serve to signify the close of the Jewish age. In Mk. 16.19-20 Mark reports that miracles, such as healings, tongue-speaking, and exorcisms, would follow those who believed (and were baptized), confirming their word as they preached. As far as how long such manifestations would continue, it is not said, either in Mk. or Ac., but their significance for the last days, the end of the Jewish age, might be taken as a clue. As we saw in Chapter Two, the rabbis taught that in the messianic age all God's people would be made prophets. This expectation of widespread prophetic powers in the messianic age was intensified by their belief that the Holy Spirit had departed Israel since the days of Haggai, Zechariah, and Malachi. So, it is possible that Peter took Joel literally and expected this work of the Spirit to continue for about two generations.

Three thousand people accepted the faith on that Pentecost. They were further entrenched in their faith by the signs and the wonders performed by the apostles' hands (vs. 43). The three thousand evidently did not receive the baptism of the Holy Spirit for at least a period of a few days, or else we would have seen some evidence that they themselves were performing miracles. Peter did not say, and there is no reason to assume, that the secondary result of immersion in water, namely, the reception of the Holy Spirit, followed immediately. All that Peter promised was that those baptized in water would sooner or later receive the same gift of the Holy Spirit which he had, along with the miraculous powers.

Another interesting passage is found in Ac. 4. Here Peter and John have been seized and imprisoned for preaching the gospel. At the consequent interrogation Peter, "filled with the Holy Spirit," spoke in such a way that the rulers of the synagogue could tell that something special was working through these uneducated followers of Jesus (vv. 5-13). Jesus had promised that the Holy Spirit would speak through his disciples at times like these (Mt. 10. 17-20, 24.19-20, Mk. 13.11, Lk. 12.11-12, 21.14-15). Peter and John were then beaten and released, at which time they returned to their brothers and sisters in the new faith. After their report, the whole group "lifted their voices together to God" (vs. 24) and prayed. "And when they had prayed, the place in which they were gathered together was shaken; and they were all filled with the Holy Spirit and spoke the word of God with boldness" (vs. 31).

As with many passages in Lk./Ac., there are many things left unsaid. For example, how is the boldness related to the possession of the Holy Spirit? One answer might be that God directly infused his disciples with boldness, or it could be rather that upon realizing that they had received the Spirit the disciples were emboldened. Certainly, at a time of great persecution and at the beginning of a great movement special motivations, like inspired prayers, would be in order.

It is also interesting to compare the "filling" of Peter in vs. 8 and the one of the disciples in vs. 31. The Greek text in vs. 8 indicates that Peter had already been filled with the Holy Spirit and that his bold and articulate speech was a present result of that past infilling. However, in vs. 31 the disciples are said to have been filled at that moment. This has led a few commentators to postulate that from Pentecost on there was one baptism, or filling, of the Holy Spirit for each convert, not repeated refillings. Thus, the disciples who received the Spirit in vs. 31 were those who had recently converted (cf. vs. 4) but had not yet received the Spirit. Peter had promised them the Spirit in Ac. 2.38; and now that promise had been fulfilled, so that the disciples were now "all" filled with the Holy Spirit.

Another highly significant passage is Ac. 8.4-25. Here Philip the Evangelist finds himself in a city of Samaria, where he preached the gospel, confirming his message with the many miracles which he performed. Enter Simon, the famous magician, who had had great influence upon the people of that area for a long time because of his magic.

> [12]But when they believed Philip as he preached good news about the kingdom of God and the name of Jesus Christ, they were baptized, both men and women. [13]Even Simon himself believed, and after being baptized he continued with Philip. And seeing signs and great miracles performed, he was amazed.
>
> [14]Now when the apostles at Jerusalem heard that Samaria had received the word of God, they sent to them Peter and John, [15]who came down and prayed for them that they might receive the Holy Spirit; [16]for it had not fallen on any of them, but they had only been baptized in the name of the Lord Jesus. [7]Then they laid their hands on them and they received the Holy Spirit. [18]Now when Simon saw that the Spirit was given through the laying on of the apostles' hands, he offered them money, saying, [19]"Give me also this power, that any one on whom I lay my hands may receive the Holy Spirit."

Peter rebuked Simon and called upon him to repent, to which Simon apparently responded positively.

First, the identity of Philip is relevant here. Since the apostles all remained in Jerusalem during this persecution (8.1), this is not Philip the apostle but rather one of those who received miraculous powers as promised in 2.38. Philip's work continues the theme set out in 1.8, namely, that the apostles (and their followers) would be witnesses of Jesus' resurrection not only in Jerusalem and Judea but also in Samaria and ultimately throughout the world. Here the Holy Spirit is the actual testifier (cf. Ac. 5.32), since Philip was not an actual eyewitness to the resurrection of Jesus.

Luke makes a point out of the Samaritans' response to the gospel. Philip's miraculous signs were so powerful as to impact even the great Simon. The people believed Philip's message and were duly baptized. Attempts are sometimes made in the commentaries to minimize the genuineness of their response, even to deny that they were truly converted, but the profundity of the Samaritans' sincerity is manifested in several ways. There was much joy, and they turned from Simon to Philip. But probably even more dramatic was the fact that a group of Samaritans, who had for generations been hostile to the Jews, accepted a starkly new message and that from a Jew.

Evidently, Philip reported the good news to the apostles in Jerusalem, who promptly dispatched Peter and John. This next point is very revealing. Peter and John came down to Samaria and prayed that the Samaritans might receive the Holy Spirit; "for it had not fallen on any of them, but they had only been baptized in the name of the Lord Jesus." This statement shows that the phrases "receive the Holy Spirit," "having the Holy Spirit fall upon someone," and "being baptized with the Holy Spirit" all refer to the same thing. It also shows that baptism in the name of Jesus is not baptism in the Holy Spirit. Baptism in the name of Jesus must be water baptism. In Ac. 2.38 Peter called upon his hearers to repent and be baptized in the name of Jesus for the forgiveness of their sins. The Samaritans had done the same: they had believed the gospel, repented of their sins, and been immersed in the name of Jesus for the remission of their sins, but they had not received the Holy Spirit. When Peter promised his audience in 2.38-39 that they would receive the Holy Spirit after their immersion in water, it is very likely that they received the Spirit either by the apostles' hands or as the people did in 4.23-33. In either event, Ac. 8 is an excellent commentary on Ac. 2. Clearly, immersion in water was a command to be obeyed in order to be saved from sin, while baptism in the Holy Spirit was a promise of miraculous gifts for which one prayed and waited.

Luke places an apparent emphasis on the laying on of the apostles' hands. Philip, not being an apostle, could not bestow the gift, so that Peter and John had to be summoned for this purpose, even though the trip would take two or three days and some inconvenience on their part. However, this is how the Samaritans received the Holy Spirit. Moreover, Simon perceived this fact and offered to pay, not for the Holy Spirit, but for the power to bestow the Spirit on people through the laying on of his hands, but Peter rejected his offer. Overall, the account leads one to believe that as a rule Christians received the Holy Spirit just that way.

I stated above that attempts have often been made to minimize and even deny the genuineness of the Samaritans' response to the gospel. The reason for this is that if the Samaritans truly gave heed to the message, believed it, and submitted sincerely to baptism in the name of Jesus, then they did so without having the Holy Spirit for some time. This would mean that the reception of the Spirit is not an element in the actual conversion process of the individual, a view which is very unpopular nowadays. However, if the

Samaritans were not really Christians until the visit by Peter and John, then one might argue that their real conversion took place when they received the Holy Spirit through the laying on of the apostles' hands.

I stated above also that all the normal language for real conversion is found in this passage. The Samaritans gave heed to the message, they had much joy, they believed the good news about the kingdom of God and the name of Jesus Christ, and they were baptized in the name of Jesus. In any other passage we would take these things as conversion. Furthermore, notice that what is said of these people is said of the whole group. Should we conclude that the whole group was insincere? No, the most apparent reading of this passage is that the Samaritans became genuine Christians upon being immersed in water in the name of Jesus for the remission of their sins, even though some time passed before they received the Holy Spirit with its attendant miraculous gifts. In fact, Luke's presentation of the Holy Spirit is in keeping with the OT's. The Spirit was primarily the spirit of prophecy. It was a supplementary gift. He never traces faith back to the Spirit, and Spirit possession was not connected by Luke to higher moral living. Perhaps the only difference in Luke from the OT is that the power was generally given, not just to a few special individuals but to a whole community.

Ac. 10.1-11.18 is almost as significant to our interests as was the last passage. This passage tells the story of the conversion of Cornelius, a Gentile. The story opens with Cornelius receiving a vision instructing him to send for a man called Peter. Meanwhile, Peter is also receiving a vision in which animals unclean to Jews are repeatedly presented to him for food. Though Peter did not understand the meaning of the vision, he was instructed by the Spirit to go with the men sent to him by Cornelius. The next day, Peter, along with six Jewish-Christian brothers, made his way to Caesarea to find Cornelius and his whole household awaiting his arrival and his message. We pick up Luke's own account in 10.34.

> [34] And Peter opened his mouth and said: Truly I perceive that God shows no partiality, [35] but in every nation any one who fears him and does what is right is acceptable to him.
>
> [36] You know the word which he sent to Israel, [37] preaching good news of peace by Jesus Christ (he is Lord of all), the word which was proclaimed throughout all Judea, beginning from Galilee after the baptism which John preached: [38] how God anointed Jesus of Nazareth with the Holy Spirit and with power; how he went about doing good and healing all who were oppressed by the devil, [39] for God was with him. And we are witnesses to all that he did both in the country of the Jews and in Jerusalem. [40] They put him to death by hanging him upon a tree; but God raised him up on the third day and made him manifest; [41] not to all the people but to us who were chosen by God as witnesses, who ate and drank with him after he arose from the dead. [42] And he commanded us to preach to the people, and to testify that he is the one ordained by God to be judge of the living and the dead. [43] To him all the prophets bear witness that every one who believes in him receives forgiveness of sins through his name."
>
> [44] While Peter was saying this, the Holy Spirit fell on all who heard the word. [45] And the believers from among the circumcised who came with Peter were amazed, because the gift of the Holy Spirit had been poured out even on the Gentiles. [46] For they heard them speaking in tongues and extolling God. [47] Then Peter declared, "Can any one forbid water for baptizing these people who have received the Holy Spirit just as we have?" [48] And he commanded them to be baptized in the name of Jesus Christ. Then they asked him to remain for some days.

Chapter 11 states that the leaders of the church in Jerusalem called Peter to come and explain these unusual events which had occurred in Caesarea. The problem, of course, was that uncircumcised Gentiles, people who were not even Jewish proselytes, had entered the fellowship without the benefit of Judaism. Luke made a point out of the chronology. In explaining his actions Peter recounted the events "in order (of occurrence)" (11.5), and throughout his explanation the chronological relationships among the events were stressed. For example, he marked the very moment of the arrival of Cornelius' embassage (vs. 11).

Peter then told how he went to Cornelius and entered his house, an action forbidden as unclean to faithful Jews. Speaking of Cornelius, Peter said,

> [13]And he told us how he had seen the angel standing and saying, [14]"'Send to Joppa and bring Simon called Peter, and he will declare to you a message by which you will be saved, you and all your household." [15]As I began to speak, the Holy Spirit fell on them just as on us at the beginning. [16]And I remembered the word of the Lord, how he said, "John baptized with water, but you shall be baptized with the Holy Spirit." [17]If then God gave the same gift to them as he gave to us when we believed in the Lord Jesus Christ, who was I to withstand God?" [18]When they heard this they were silenced. And they glorified God, saying, "Then to the Gentiles also God has granted repentance unto life."

The story of Cornelius is significant to Luke, of course, in that it records how the gospel first broke into the Gentile world. Ac 11.19 states that the early church was totally Jewish up until that time. It seems that even the apostles had been reticent to preach the gospel outside of Jewry, so God took the initiative and engineered the events of the above passage.

It is interesting to note in passing, that Peter was perplexed by the vision, even though he saw it three times. Here was a man possessed of the Spirit, yet he was not able to understand its import. It seems that prophets in biblical literature were at no special advantage but rather were in the same position as others who heard a revelation described, that is, as part of the audience. Visions and revelations, though private, were still not to be subjectively understood. It would take the events at Cornelius' house to objectively interpret the vision to Peter.

(Peter's sermon to Cornelius included a reference to Jesus' having been anointed by the Spirit. This would appear to be a reference to the events surrounding Jesus' baptism. From that time on Jesus was a prophet and a miracle-worker. We might also note the witness theme again.)

While Peter was preaching, the Holy Spirit fell on Cornelius' household. In vv. 44-47 the following relevant phrases were used interchangeably by Luke: "the Holy Spirit fell on them," "the gift of the Holy Spirit was poured out on them," "they received the Holy Spirit," and in 11.16 "they were baptized with the Holy Spirit." Once again we find no distinctions among such phrases; they are simply different ways of describing the same thing.

The baptism of the Holy Spirit was made evident by tongue-speaking. Evidently, Cornelius and his Latin/Greek-speaking household were suddenly and miraculously speaking in Hebrew or Aramaic, for Peter's Jewish friends understood what they were saying and were amazed that they were fluently speaking in a tongue heretofore foreign to them. Notice, incidentally, that the substance of the tongue-speaking was the glorification of God (comp. Ac. 2.11).

Also, once again, we find Luke using "baptism in the name of Jesus" virtually as a technical term for water baptism (Ac. 2 and 8). Cornelius and his family had already received the Holy Spirit; now they were to be immersed in water.

Chapter 11 provides some very informative commentary on the events of chapter 10. As I have already pointed out, the chronological order of the events is very important to Luke, an aspect of Luke's account which is also very helpful to us. Luke's point is that things happened in such a way and in such an order as to compel Peter along the course he took; he really had no choice other than to do what he did. Similarly, we find in vs. 14 that Cornelius waited in his home for Peter, expecting to hear a message from the latter by which he and his household would be saved. In other words, Cornelius would have to receive Peter, hear and understand the message, and respond positively to that message before he could be saved, but in fact the Holy Spirit fell on Cornelius as Peter *began* to speak (vs. 15), for Luke used the Greek word for "began" which literally means "first of" or "at the top of" the story. Cornelius could not have heard enough of Peter's message to make a responsible decision at the moment when the Holy Spirit fell on him. This means that Cornelius and his household received the Holy Spirit and spoke in tongues *before* they were saved. That fact is remarkable. Coupled with the account of the Samaritans in Ac. 8, the Cornelius account makes it clear that baptism in the Holy Spirit was not a part of a person's salvation experience. Mostly, it seems, people received the Holy Spirit after being saved, but in Cornelius' case it occurred before salvation. The reason for this, given Luke's emphasis, would have to be that it served to confirm Peter's impression that Gentiles who accepted Jesus should be accepted into the Body of Christ without their having to submit to Jewish rites and laws. Peter's rhetorical question makes this point: "If then God gave the same gift to them as he gave to us when we believed in the Lord Jesus Christ, who was I to withstand God?" Once again we find the work of the Holy Spirit to be confirmatory, testifying to man of God's will. In fact, the Cornelius episode became something of a controversy in the early church, and later at Jerusalem Peter argued from the baptism of the Holy Spirit to the justification of his including the household of Cornelius in the kingdom (Ac. 15.7-9):

[7]And after there had been considerable debate, Peter rose and said

to them, "Brethren, you know that in the early days God made a choice among you, that by my mouth the Gentiles should hear the word of the gospel and believe. [8]And God who knows the heart bore witness to them, giving them the Holy Spirit just as he did to us; [9]and he made no distinction between us and them, but cleansed their hearts by faith.

Peter's concluding remark surfaces one final point. Peter said that Cornelius had received the same gift he and the apostles had received at Pentecost. As we saw in Ac. 2, the nature of that gift was not salvific, but rather prophetic, equipping the receivers of it for the work of the ministry and also serving as a sign. Such was the case here with Cornelius.

Our final major passage from the works of Luke is found in Ac. 18.24-19.7. In this story an Alexandrian Jew named Apollos had come to Ephesus. Though he was a disciple of Jesus, he had never been baptized into the name of Jesus but had received only John's baptism. Now John the baptizer had been dead for over twenty years. Either Apollos had received John's baptism at that time, or he had been baptized later by one of John's disciples. Then, after that, Apollos learned that the Messiah was Jesus, learned many things about the teachings of this Jesus, and became an ardent disciple. In Ephesus Apollos encountered Priscilla and Aquila, who corrected his error about baptism and no doubt baptized him in the name of Jesus the Messiah. Later, Apollos joined the work in Corinth.

[19.1] While Apollos was at Corinth, Paul passed through the upper country and came to Ephesus. There he found some disciples. [2]And he said to them, "Did you receive the Holy Spirit when you believed?" And they said, "No, we have never even heard that there is a Holy Spirit." [3]And he said, "Into what then were you baptized?" They said, "Into John's Baptism." [4]And Paul said, "John baptized with the baptism of repentance, telling the people to believe in the one who was to come after him, that is, Jesus." [5]On hearing this, they were baptized in the name of the Lord Jesus. [6]And when Paul had laid his hands upon them, the Holy Spirit came on them; and they spoke with tongues and prophesied. ⁷There were about twelve of them in all.

Paul's query as to whether the Ephesian dozen had received the Holy Spirit indicates that the possession of the Spirit was a general phenomenon among converts in the early church. Here were some disciples; surely, Paul must have thought, they had the Spirit. Perhaps Paul had noticed a conspicuous absence of charismata, and so, perplexed, he questioned them. Now, John the Baptizer was a prophet himself, having the Spirit in him, but he expressly declared that whereas he baptized people only with water the Messiah would do more than that, namely, baptize people also with the Holy Spirit.

Once again we find that pattern so consistent in the Book of Acts: water baptism had to do with the remission of sins, and Spirit-baptism had to do with the reception of charismata. In fact, as we saw in our discussion of Ac. 8 above, baptism in the name of the Lord Jesus was immersion in water in order to receive forgiveness of sins; baptism in the Holy Spirit was something else. There are those who have argued that the two are the same and that the reception of the Holy Spirit is essential to conversion, so that in Ac. 8 we must conclude that the Samaritans had not genuinely converted to Christ until they received the Spirit. However, Ac. 19 shows that Luke knew very well how to deal with defective conversions and baptisms. If the Samaritans had not been genuine, or at best confused, Peter would have rebaptized them, the latter time in the name of the Lord Jesus, as did Paul the Ephesian dozen.

In our examination of the Book of Acts we have concentrated on the following major passages, Ac. 1-2, 4, 8, 10-11, and 19. These indeed are the boldest and clearest of Luke's statements about the function of the Spirit in the early church, though there are many other minor allusions to the Spirit. Throughout Acts the general picture is that Spirit-possession means having miraculous power, especially prophecy. The Spirit primarily served to confirm Christianity through signs and wonders, but it also gave the apostles speech in times of great stress, it guided them in their mission work through visions, it inspired prophets with predictions about the future, and it empowered elders and evangelists for their work.

CHAPTER FIVE

THE HOLY SPIRIT IN THE WRITINGS OF JOHN

Though not without some controversy, tradition has attributed the apostle John with five of the books found in the NT: the gospel, the three letters, and the Book of Revelation, the last of which we shall take up first.

The Book of Revelation was written much in the same style as was Ezekiel, Daniel, Zechariah, I Enoch, Jubilees, and other such apocalyptic works. In our survey of rabbinic apocalyptic works in Chapter Two we found several allusions to the Holy Spirit, as we will also in Revelation.

First of all, we come across the phrase, "I was in the Spirit" (1.10, 4.2, 17.3, and 21.10), which in each case introduces a visionary experience. We find the same phrase in Jewish intertestamental literature, each time referring to a prophet under the Spirit's control, as evidenced by a visionary experience, ecstatic speech, and/or a revelation. Clearly, being in the Spirit is prophetic.

Secondly, the Spirit is even an active character in the visions, carrying on conversations with John. In 2.7, 11, 17, 29, 3.6, 13, and 22 the phrase is repeated, "He who has an ear, let him hear what the Spirit says to the churches." The Spirit is thus warning churches of impending judgment, if they do not repent. Similarly, in another vision, the Spirit pronounces a blessing on the dead who die in the Lord (14.13). And finally, in 22.17: "The Spirit and the Bride say, 'Come.'"

There are several other references to spirit in the Revelation, but they are of highly doubtful significance to a study of the Holy Spirit. There are, for example, evil spirits (foul spirits and demonic spirits), the seven spirits of God (an image probably taken from Jewish literature to refer to God's omnipresence), God's breath, the spirit of prophecy, and the spirits of the prophecy. As we said, none of these has anything to do with the Holy Spirit.

We come next to I John, the only one of the three letters which has any reference to the Spirit, the main one of which will be provided in full (3.19-4.13).

[19]By this we shall know that we are of the truth, [20]and reassure our hearts before him whenever our hearts condemn us; for God is greater than our hearts, and he knows everything. [21]Beloved, if our hearts do not condemn us, we have confidence before God; [22]and we receive from him whatever we ask, because we keep his commandments and do what pleases him. [23]And this is his commandment, that we should believe in the name of his Son Jesus Christ and love one another, just as he has commanded us. [24]All who keep his commandments abide in him, and he in them. And by this we know that he abides in us, by the spirit which he has given us.

[4.1]Beloved, do not believe every spirit, but test the spirits to see whether they are from God; for many false prophets have gone out into the world. [2]By this you know the spirit of God: every spirit which confesses that Jesus Christ has come in the flesh is of God, [3]and every spirit which does not confess Jesus is not of God. This is the spirit of antichrist, of which you heard that it was coming, and now it is in the world already.

[4]Little children, you are of God, and have overcome them; for he who is in you is greater than he who is in the world. [5]They are of the world, therefore what they say is of the world, and the world listens to them. [6]We are of God. Whoever knows God listens to us, and he who is not of God does not listen to us. By this we know the spirit of truth and the spirit of error.

[7]Beloved, let us love one another; for love is of God, and he who loves is born of God and knows God. [8]He who does not love does not know God; for God is love. [9]In this the love

of God was made manifest among us, that God sent his only Son into the world, so that we might live through him. ¹⁰In this is love, not that we loved God but that he loved us and sent his Son to be the expiation for our sins. ¹¹Beloved, if God so loved us, we ought to love one another. ¹²No man has ever seen God; if we love one another, God abides in us, and his love is perfected in us.
¹³By this we know that we abide in him and he in us, because he has given us of his own Spirit. ¹⁴And we have seen his Son the Savior of the world. ¹⁵Whoever confesses that Jesus is the Son of God, God abides in him, and he in God.

The occasion for the writing of I Jn. is widely regarded to be the threat of a heresy very much like some of the gnostic heresies later described by Ireneaus. John was dealing with a style of intellectual elitism which generated a profligacy of sin on the one hand and superspirituality on the other. Either result was unloving and created divisions between brothers in the faith. The confusion had evidently led some of John's readers to doubt their own spiritual security. So John wrote them to rectify these problems.

The mark of a true Christian, he said, was brotherly love. By this the Christian could know that he was of the truth. Another important sign of the true believer was faith in the actual physical life, death, and resurrection of Jesus. And a third was a general obedience to the moral precepts that Jesus had preached. Hence, in 3.24 John said that his readers would know that God abode in them by the spirit He had given to them. At this point "spirit" could mean attitude or character: a faith in Jesus which led to a love of the brethren and an obedient attitude toward the moral precepts was the spirit they had learned from God. In fact, the language is very much like that of the Dead Sea Scrolls where the hymnists thanked God for the spirit (or spirits) which God had given them. They apparently meant the attitudes of holiness, mercy, understanding, and justice.

They also mentioned the Holy Spirit, but, as we saw, that was something additional. Given the connection between gnosticism and the Dead Sea Scrolls, as well as John's use of their terminology, the most likely conclusion is that John in I Jn. 3.24 referred to a godly attitude.

However, 4.1-13 would appear to change that interpretation. John wanted his readers to test the spirits to see whether they were of God. "Spirit" here seems to be synonymous with "prophet" in these verses. In fact, this passage could provide us with a linguistic case of metonymy, that is, a figure of speech whereby a word is put for its operations. On this view, John wanted spirits (prophets) tested with regard to the physical nature of Jesus. If the spirit agreed that Jesus had come in the flesh, then he was a spirit of God. The reference to the spirit of God in 4.2 probably does not mean the Holy Spirit, but rather the spirit (prophet) truly sent from God. Of course, such a prophet would be inspired by the Holy Spirit, and perhaps the Holy Spirit was the one John said was in them (4.4).

One would think, however, that there could have been false prophets who did not reject Jesus' having come in the flesh but taught other false doctrines instead. How then could Jesus' physicality provide the necessary test? The answer must be that all of John's remarks were restricted to that particular heresy which was circulating at that time. John called that heresy (or the entity which promoted that heresy) "the spirit of antichrist," which had already come into the world (cf. 2.18-25). So, in light of this controversy, current in John's time, the question of Jesus' physicality distinguished the spirit of truth from the spirit of error (4.6). The language here is very similar to that of the Dead Sea Scrolls, where such spirits were principles of good and evil.

John then returned to one of the surest tests of a true prophet: does his teaching promote genuine love? He set forth the basic gospel message of God's love for sinners and how that should motivate Christians to love one another. God had given them of His own nature the principle of love. He had given it to them in the gospel.

It must be admitted, though, that a few of the "spirit" occurrences might refer to the Holy Spirit. The Spirit in 3.24 could be just such an example. The Spirit in Christians was a way of knowing that they had fellowship with God. Parallel language can be found in 2.18-29. There John spoke of the antichrists having come, denying the Son. In contrast to this, John's audience had been anointed by the Holy One, so that they were able to know the truth and not be deceived. In fact, this anointing taught them everything they needed to know. Putting the two passages together, we might say that John's audience had the gifts of prophecy and discernment given them by the Holy Spirit, by which they were taught the truth, and that he was encouraging them to listen to their established prophets and not to be turned aside from the truth by imposters.

Similarly, in 4.13-15 John might have been referring to the prophetic and miraculous gifts of the Holy Spirit. The remark about seeing and testifying (witnessing) would lend credence to this interpretation. John's point, then, in 4.7-15 would be that on the basis of these signs of the Holy Spirit they should know that Jesus came in the flesh and died for them, teaching them a new dimension of love.

Our last passage from I Jn. is 5.6-8:

> This is he who came by water and blood, Jesus Christ, not with the water only but with the water and the blood. ⁷And the Spirit is the witness, because the Spirit is the truth. ⁸There are three witnesses, the Spirit, the water, and the blood; and these three agree.

Interpretations abound on this passage. I agree with the majority view on verse 6. The water refers to Jesus' baptism and the blood refers to his crucifixion. John was responding to the current gnostic-type heresy that a divine entity could not be in mortal flesh. John's response was that not only was Jesus the Messiah (the Son of God) in his baptism but also in his death. The reference in these verses is probably to the Holy Spirit in its usual witness role, confirming the genuineness of Jesus with miracles and prophecy.

With that we turn to the Gospel of John. Our first occurrence of the Holy Spirit is in 1:29-34, where John has baptized Jesus. As we saw in the other gospel accounts, the Spirit descended in the form of a dove, however, John does not add much with regard to the Spirit here.

There are several major passages on the Holy Spirit in John's gospel, though, and 3.1-12 is one of them, where Jesus received a visit from Nicodemus. The latter had trouble understanding Jesus' reference to a second birth, or a birth from above, as the correct translation may be, but Jesus explained by restating his point:

> [5]Truly, truly, I say to you, unless one is born of water and of the spirit, he cannot enter the kingdom of God. [6]That which is born of the flesh is flesh, and that which is born of the Spirit is spirit. Do not marvel that I said to you, "You must be born anew." [8]The wind blows where it wills, and you hear the sound of it, but you do not know whence it comes or whither it goes; so it is with every one who is born of the Spirit.

The new birth has received a great deal of attention, even though the expression is relatively rare in the NT. The phrase "born anew" can be translated equally well as "born from above," and the contrast between above and below explicitly emerges in vv. 12-3. Jesus therefore could very well have been talking about the nature, rather than the temporal order, of the two births. Furthermore, Jesus also referred to this birth as a birth of water and the Spirit. It is possible that flesh and spirit are qualities here, so that Jesus was speaking of one's being born of spirit, not *the* Spirit. The difference between flesh as a quality and spirit as a quality seems to find clarification in Jesus' wordplay on the word "spirit." As we noted in the first chapter of this book, "spirit" is often appropriately translated "wind." So, spirit is like the wind; one can see its effects but not much else. One could see miracles (a matter under discussion, vs. 2), but one could not understand them fully. So, "spirit" here could be either the Holy Spirit or the quality of spirit versus the quality of flesh. This kind of contrast has occurred before. Isaiah said that the Egyptians' horses were, unlike God, flesh, not spirit (31.3). Similarly, this distinction can be found in the Dead Sea Scrolls, the Jewish philosopher Philo, as well as in Mt. 26.41, Mk. 14.38, and Lk. 22.46. When this contrast is made, it is not the Holy Spirit which is involved; rather it is the realm of the non-physical. To be born of the spirit, then, is to experience a new beginning, not a new physical beginning, but rather a new beginning in life and in state of mind.

Neither was Jesus talking about the baptism of the Holy Spirit. There is no mention of this baptism, and we have already seen in other contexts that the baptism of the Holy Spirit had to do with the receipt of miraculous powers. Indeed, historically, the birth of water and spirit was understood by the early church as immersion in water for the remission of sins until the time of John Calvin.

So, these considerations lead me to the conclusion that Jesus in Jn. 3 was speaking of spirit in the sense of spirituality as opposed to fleshliness and that this passage is not about the Holy Spirit at all.

Next, we come to Jn. 3.31-35, where the author of the gospel apparently embellished his narrative with an interpretive aside. In this passage John compared the ministries of John the Baptizer and Jesus.

> [31]He who comes from above is above all; he who is of the earth belongs to the earth, and of the earth he speaks; he who comes from heaven is above all. [32]He bears witness to what he has seen and heard, yet no one receives his testimony; [33] he who receives his testimony sets his seal to this, that God is true. [34]For he whom God has sent utters the words of God, for it is not by measure that he gives the Spirit; [35]the Father loves the Son, and has given all things into his hand.

As in the last passage, we find here the earth/heaven distinction and the recalcitrance of the earthly mind. Jesus is of heaven, sent by God. He is a prophet and testifies of heavenly truths, truths which could not be known otherwise. "For it is not by measure that he gives the Spirit." The context demands that "he" is God. Notice vs. 35: the Father gives all things to the Son. So, John's point was that the Father gave the Spirit to the Son and gave him all of it.

In previous passages we have come across the notion of measures of the Spirit. In Nu. 11.16-30, for example, God took some of the spirit which was upon Moses and put it on the seventy elders. Elisha asked Elijah for a double portion of his spirit (II K 2.9). In the Dead Sea Scrolls the two spirits struggle for dominance in each human breast and exist there in double measure. The rabbis discussed how the Holy Spirit rested on various prophets in various degrees of weight, and some wondered if Moses had not lost some in Nu. 11, as did Philo also. So, the idea has to do with the degree of influence of the Spirit. John, therefore, was saying that Jesus enjoyed the maximum influence of the Holy Spirit. In the context this means that he was a prophet in the fullest possible measure. Nothing that would have been given to any prophet was held back from him. Even though John the Baptizer was a great prophet, he was eclipsed by Jesus. For that reason, one's response to his message had everything to do with one's receiving eternal life. Also, as is often pointed out, Jesus was even more than the greatest prophet, he was the one who would baptize with the Spirit as well.

We next come to the story of the Samaritan woman at Jacob's well in Jn. 4, where we find a woman made uncomfortable by Jesus' penetrating questions, from which she conveniently changed the subject from her personal situation to a contemporary theological controversy. The Samaritans had worshiped for some time on Mt. Gerazim, while the Jews went to Mt. Zion in Jerusalem, the result of a contention between the two groups which went back, in fact, to the division of the kingdom in 928 B.C. Jesus replied that the Jews were right, but that that was all about to change (Jn. 4.21-24).

> [21]Jesus said to her, "Woman, believe me, the hour is coming when neither on this mountain nor in Jerusalem will you worship the Father. [22]You worship what you do not know; we worship what we know, for salvation is of the Jews. [23]But the hour is coming, and now is, when the true worshipers will worship the Father in spirit and truth, for such the Father seeks to worship him. [24]God is spirit, and those who worship him must worship him in spirit and truth."

Now, Jesus' remarks about spirit and truth must be interpreted in this context. His point must have involved, at least, the claim that location was about to cease to be important to worship. God's nature lay at the bottom of all of this. God is spirit. In secular Greek, as we saw in Chapter Two above, God was often characterized as being spirit. The Stoics especially are said to have fixed the essence of God as intelligent, fiery air, or spirit, which pervades the universe, but without having a form, analogous to soul. A later Stoic, Seneca, called God "that celestial spirit." However, on one occasion we do have something similar to this in the OT; in Is. 31.3 God is said to be spirit and not flesh. It is possible, then, that John has been influenced by Greek thinking; but the OT influence, though slight, is the more probable, since John nowhere appears to view God as some metaphysical element of the universe, but instead just the opposite, spirit as opposed to the physical flesh. So, in the context of Jn. 4 Jesus was saying that God is not physical. God is not constrained by space or location. Accordingly, those who worship God are not constrained by space or location. Mountains for worship have been transcended by a more ultimate sense of worship; God is now to be worshiped with the mind, not with a physical ritual in a specific location.

Similarly, in Jn. 6.63, where Jesus said, "It is the spirit that gives life, the flesh is no avail; the words that I have spoken to you are spirit and life," it is not the Holy Spirit which is under discussion. Rather, Jesus was simply contrasting his spiritual food with the physical manna Moses had given to the Israelites in the wilderness.

In Jn. 7.37-39, though, we find the following:

> [37]On the last day of the feast, the great day, Jesus stood up and proclaimed,[38]"If any one thirst, let him come to me and drink. He who believes in me, as the scripture has said, 'Out of his heart shall flow rivers of living water.'" [39]Now this he said about the Spirit, which those who believe in him were to receive; for as yet the Spirit had not been given, because Jesus was not yet glorified.

There is no one particular OT passage which corresponds to Jesus' reference. Numerous passages relate salvation or God's grace to water, though. Is. 44.1-5 not only uses this metaphor but also associates it with God pouring out his Spirit on the Jews. Jesus therefore had some basis for saying that the OT had made that association.

Jesus also often spoke of how his hour had not yet come (Jn. 2.4, 7.6, 30, 8.20), but after the triumphant entry into Jerusalem he knew that that hour had come (12.27). It was an hour of anguish. When he dismissed Judas, he said that the time of his glorification had come (13.31-32). Obviously, the hour of his glorification was the event of his crucifixion and the resurrection. That means that the Spirit was not given until after Jesus' death. Of course, many received the Spirit in the OT, and the disciples had received the power to exorcise demons (Mt. 10.6), so John must have had a specific dispensation of the Spirit in mind. As we saw in Ac. 2, the Jews expected the messianic age to be ushered in with a great outpouring of the Spirit. The rabbis expected the same. Hence, the outpouring of the Holy Spirit on the day of Pentecost in Ac. 2 is the best candidate for the event about which John spoke in 7.39.

It is tempting at this point to associate the water of baptism with the baptism of the Holy Spirit, but we should resist that temptation. The context of Jn. 7 is the Jewish Feast of Tabernacles. During that feast water taken from the Pool of Siloam in a golden pitcher was included in the morning sacrifice, the significance of which was the water God had miraculously supplied during the wilderness wanderings and the streams which were to issue from the temple in the Messianic Age. Just as Isaiah also did, Jesus associated the outpouring of the Holy Spirit, which was to occur shortly thereafter, with the quenching of parched land by a welcomed downpour of rain. It is a baptism for sure, but it has nothing to do with immersion in water in the name of Jesus for the remission of sins.

There are two more major passages on the Holy Spirit in the Gospel of John. One is the three-chapter section called The Olivet Discourse (chapters 13-16), and the other is chapter 20, verses 21-23. First The Olivet Discourse.

At the last supper Jesus' main concern was the viability of his mission after he left it in the hands of his disciples. He was concerned about their understanding of his message, their unity, and their continued faithfulness under certain persecution. This section opens with Jesus washing the feet of the disciples, an action aimed at dramatizing and emphasizing the essentiality of a spirit of humble servanthood. Then after dismissing Judas Iscariot to do his work, Jesus began to prepare his disciples for his own departure.

In the course of his warm, reassuring remarks to his disciples Jesus mentioned the miracles he had performed in their midst as evidence that he really was the Son of God. However, he continued, they would do even greater works, in fact whatever they might come to ask in his name (14.12-14). Jesus then added, "And I will pray the Father, and he will give you another Counselor, to be with you for ever, even the Spirit of truth, whom the world cannot receive, because it neither sees him nor knows him; you know him, for he dwells with you, and will be in you" (14.16-17). This is our first occurrence of the Holy Spirit as a counselor (vs. 26 identifies this counselor with the Holy Spirit). Other translations put helper, comforter, and paraclete, but the exact meaning of the original Greek term is notoriously obscure. It comes from classical Greek, where it means legal assistant or advocate, or sometimes intercessor, but even though the Holy Spirit is set in a legal setting at least once (Mk. 13.11) and is said to be an intercessor (Ro. 8.26), this sense does not appear to be the one found here in John. I personally lean toward the meaning of comforter. The messianic age was characterized by, among other things, God's comfort (Is. 40.1 and Mt. 5.4), and the prophetic message of the apostles and early disciples was also seen as comforting (Ac. 2.40 and I Co. 14.3 in the Greek). Hence, the work of the Holy Spirit, inspiring these early Christians with the prophetic word led to the view of the Holy Spirit as The Comforter.

Jesus also mentioned that the Holy Spirit would be with his disciples forever (14.16). This point has led many to conclude that Jesus intended the Spirit to be a possession of each disciple in every age, but we need to be careful with that assumption. This was not an unusual hebraism. In Dt. 15.12-18 a freed slave might ask to remain a slave in his master's house even after the master had offered him his freedom. If the master agreed to keep him as a slave, he would bore a hole in the slave's ear, and the slave would belong to the master *forever*. So, unlike Jesus in the flesh, the Holy Spirit would never leave those disciples; the Spirit would be with *them* forever.

One of the main themes of the Olivet Discourse is the necessity of continued faithfulness. Again and again Jesus returned to this point (14.15, 21, 23-24, 15.1-11, 14, and 16.1-4). In fact, the receipt of the Holy Spirit would be contingent upon the disciples' continued obedience. Their faithfulness would not be enough in itself, but without it the gift of the Holy Spirit would be meaningless. So, Jesus promised them that they would be given the Spirit to help them carry on his mission. Apparently, there was a connection between the greater works of 14.12-14 and the gift of the Spirit. I suggest that Jesus was not talking about the Holy Spirit helping the disciples live faithful lives, but rather that *if* they remained faithful they would receive the additional help needed to do works in Jesus' name, even greater works than he did. This circumstance would not be unusual in the prophetic tradition of the Bible. There were similar tandem relationships between Moses and Joshua and Elijah and Elisha. Understood in this sense, Jesus was passing on the Spirit to his disciples to carry out the same work, attended by similar miraculous signs. Unlike "the world," which is not obedient to God, it would be necessary that the disciples *were* obedient so that they might receive the Spirit.

But how is it that the Holy Spirit dwelt *with* the disciples, but would soon dwell *in* them (14.17)? I believe this is explained in the ensuing verses where Jesus promises them that he would not leave them desolate but that he would come to them. The world would see him no more, but his chosen disciples would see him (14.18-19). Thus, Jesus identifies himself very closely with the Spirit. He himself was with them at the time of his speaking these words, but soon he (in the mode of the Holy Spirit) would be in them.

Jesus then proceeded to give them two ways that the Spirit would function in their lives (14.26),

> But the Counselor, the Holy Spirit, whom the Father will send in my name, he will teach you all things, and bring to your remembrance all that I have said to you.

That is, they would be prophetically inspired. It is easy to see why these gifts would be important. Jesus was physically leaving, but they would not be left to their own raw abilities and devices to carry on his work. It is at this point that it becomes so very clear that this passage is not about discipleship in all ages, but rather that it is about the specific conditions surrounding the special task of these disciples and the stresses of their situation. The indwelling Holy Spirit would displace that special circumstance of Jesus' physical presence, it would teach them things which they were not ready to understand, and it would give them a secure memory of the things Jesus had taught them while he was with them, as Jesus stated later (15.26),

> But when the Counselor comes, whom I shall send to you from the Father, even the Spirit of truth, who proceeds from the Father, he will bear witness to me; and you also are witnesses, because

you have been with me from the beginning".

Jesus then spoke again about the impending persecution and his concern that his disciples not fall away and then concluded (16.4b-5),

> I did not say these things to you from the beginning, because I was with you. But now I am going to him who sent me; . . . .

And then (vv. 7-11),

> Nevertheless I tell you the truth; it is to your advantage that I go away, for if I do not go away, the Counselor will not come to you; but if I go, I will send him to you. ⁸And when he comes, he will convince the world of sin and righteousness and judgment: ⁹of sin because they do not believe in me; ¹⁰of righteousness, because I go to the Father, and you will see me no more; ¹¹of judgment, because the ruler of this world is judged.

Why it was necessary that Jesus depart so that the Spirit might come is not clear, but it is the same as John said in 7.37-40. Furthermore, the Spirit's job would be to convince (convict) the world of sin, righteousness, and judgment. Neither did Jesus say how the counselor would carry out its task, but, given the context here, it would presumably be through the apostles' inspired preaching.

The final paragraph (16.12-14) in Jesus' remarks is more instructive.

> I have yet many things to say to you, but you cannot bear them now. ¹³When the Spirit of truth comes, he will guide you into all the truth; for he will not speak on his own authority, but whatever he hears he will speak, and he will declare to you the things that are to come. He will glorify me, for he will take what is mine and declare it to you. ¹⁴All that the Father has is mine; therefore I said that he will take what is mine and declare it to you.

These words show again how Jesus' remarks about the Holy Spirit have to do with the concerns of the apostles and their mission and not with the concerns of twentieth century disciples. The disciples had had great difficulty with Jesus' concept of the Kingdom, his statements about his death, and his promise of his resurrection. It was not until they saw the empty tomb that they were able to begin to put things together (20.8-9), still less so at this point. There was only so much that they could handle at this stage in their understanding. They would get the whole message, "all the truth," but only after they had received the Holy Spirit. The complete message would also include future events; Jesus here was speaking of predictive prophecy. And finally, notice how the work of the Spirit here was in terms of things which would be "declared." Again, this is prophecy, not moral empowerment or any other kind of work.

Chapters fourteen through sixteen are so important to an understanding of John's view of the Spirit that a summary of their contents is called for at his point.

1) The disciples' possession of the Holy Spirit is probably to be understood as a temporary phenomenon.
    a) The context is that of the period of persecution following the birth of the Christian movement.
    b) The Spirit would give the disciples a remembrance of the things Jesus had said to them.
    c) The Spirit would fill in those gaps left there by their inability to grasp the whole story.
    d) The Spirit would be a witness alongside the disciples to the life, death, and resurrection of Jesus.

2) The Spirit was referred to variously:
   a) the Counselor (Comforter, Helper, Paraclete),
   b) the Spirit of truth, and
   c) the Holy Spirit.
3) The Spirit would be sent them from the Father.
4) The Spirit would empower the disciples to do even greater works than Jesus did.
5) The disciples' receipt of the Spirit was contingent upon their continued faithfulness and obedience.
6) The Spirit evidently was seen as a replacement for Jesus.
7) The Spirit would dwell in the disciples.
8) The functions of the Spirit would include the following:
   a) He would teach the disciples everything they would need to know.
   b) He would give them a remembrance of Jesus' teachings.
   c) He would bear witness to Jesus (apparently through miraculous works).
   d) He would convict the world of sin, righteousness, and judgment.
   e) He would reveal future events.

Finally, we come to Jn. 20.21-23, an enigmatic passage which records one of the appearances Jesus made to his disciples after his resurrection from the dead.

> Jesus said to them again, "Peace be with you. As the Father has sent me, even so I send you." [22]And when he had said this, he breathed on them, and said to them, "Receive the Holy Spirit. [23]If you forgive the sins of any, they are forgiven; if you retain the sins of any, they are retained.

In this passage there are several points of contact with the lengthy discourse we just treated. Jesus had gone away; now he is back. He promised them peace; now he blesses them. He had stated that the disciples would be witnesses to him and do even greater works than he had done; he now breathes upon them and bestows the Spirit. Even so, this is a rather strange passage. At least four questions rise to the surface:

1) What is the background which explains this text?
2) What did Jesus bestow upon the disciples?
3) What was the purpose of the breathing and the endowment?
4) How does this event relate to the Pentecost event?

As for the first question, most commentators refer to Gn. 2.7 and Ezk. 37.9-10 in the LXX, where this rare Greek word for breathing is used for breathing life. The implication would be that Jesus was breathing life into the disciples, or into their ministry, or maybe even that the disciples were being converted. However, given the fact that the disciples were already alive and that this metaphor is used nowhere else for conversion, another interpretation should be preferred. The most interesting suggestion which I have come across is that we have here a very primitive memory of Jesus' actual words in his original Aramaic. If so, then by turning to Gn. 2.7 in the Targums (in all of the basic sources) we will find that there the reference is to Adam's acquisition of the faculty of speech (cf. pp. 30-31 above). On this interpretation, Jesus' breathing upon the disciples served as a symbolic action with reference to their impending prophetic powers.

As for the second question, the question revolves around whether Jesus bestowed the Holy Spirit or something else. Some have asserted that Jesus gave his disciples a gift of the Holy Spirit, not the Holy Spirit itself

-- in fact, Jesus' holy spirit. However, if that were the case, it would be indeed a very rare usage, and the grammatical arguments which have been marshaled in its favor are very unimpressive. Instead, the context of the whole Book of John argues for a reference to the Holy Spirit here. In Jn. 1.29-34 the Spirit came down upon Jesus as a dove, authorizing Jesus to baptize in the Holy Spirit. In 3.34 Jesus received the Spirit, empowering him to be the prophet par excellence. In 7.38-39 Jesus promised the Spirit to believers after his glorification. And in chs. 14-16 Jesus again promised the Holy Spirit to his disciples after his departure. With all of this in mind, Jn. 20.22 should be understood as a passage about the receipt of the Holy Spirit itself. Just as Jesus received the Holy Spirit to empower him as a prophet and missionary, so also would the disciples soon receive the same.

The third question has to do with the purpose behind Jesus' actions, and to that question I would respond that Jesus was commissioning his disciples. That interpretation would certainly fit the context. The theme of chs. 14-16 is that Jesus would send the disciples the Holy Spirit as a Paraclete to help them carry out their work as witnesses. In Jn. 20 Jesus explicitly sent the disciples out. Notice also the parallel between vs. 23 and Mt. 18.18: each passage bespeaks of the apostolic authority the disciples were now assuming. Finally, as we discussed under the second question, the prophetic speech Jesus offered would equip the disciples for their roles as witnesses.

The fourth question is the most difficult. How does this account in Jn. square with Luke's account of the Pentecost in Ac. 2? Many suggestions have been offered. As we saw above, some deny that Jesus here bestowed the Holy Spirit. Some suggest that any attempts at harmonizing the two accounts are misguided. Others have suggested that the giving of the Spirit was progressive, that its powers came in stages.

An old view, one held by Theodore of Mopsuestia and John Calvin, is that Jn. 20 is proleptic, that is, anticipatory of Ac. 2. In other words, Jesus performed a ritualistic breathing, symbolizing the baptism of the Holy Spirit soon to come upon the disciples. After all, as is commonly pointed out by commentators today, John's gospel does often reflect a more primitive character than do the other gospels. John therefore is here telling the story the way it happened. John also reflects some influence of Hellenistic thinking. Nowhere in the OT do we find God bestowing the Holy Spirit upon people by breathing upon them, but in Graeco-Roman literature we do. As we saw in Chapter Two, on numerous occasions in Graeco-Roman writings deities breathed upon people empowering them with prophetic powers, poetic abilities, and superhuman powers. The effects would not have to be immediate either. So, Jesus was not actually bestowing the Holy Spirit upon the disciples in John's account, rather he was indicating in his typical indirect way that he was God. The breathing ritual was symbolic and promissory. We saw under Jn. 14-16 that the elements of that discourse were parallel to the elements of Lk. 24-Ac. 2. How could John be that explicitly accurate in one passage and glibly ignore those details in another? And in John's account Thomas was not even present to receive the Spirit. No, Jn. 20 is a proleptic reference to the miraculous powers, especially inspired speech, which the disciples were to receive on Pentecost.

In conclusion we note that John's references to the Holy Spirit have had to do with miraculous endowments. As for the baptism of the Holy Spirit, John is in basic agreement with the synoptic evangelists, even though his language and presentation are different. Jesus baptized people in water (Jn 4.1ff) just as John the Baptizer did; but as the Messiah he would baptize people also in the Holy Spirit. This baptism of the Holy Spirit would not occur, though, until after his death upon the cross. The rebirth of water and spirit, of which Jesus spoke to Nicodemus, had no particular connection with the baptism of the Holy Spirit; instead, the baptism of the Holy Spirit is best understood in light of the promises Jesus made to the disciples at the last supper. The baptism of the Holy Spirit was the Spirit working miracles through the apostles and revealing prophetic messages to them.

One fairly distinctive trait of John's writings is the way he contraposed flesh and spirit and sometimes referred to spirit as a quality which characterized the nature of God. In so doing, John called his readers to rise above the fleshly sphere of existence. John's Gospel makes it clear that many passages which mention spirit are not about the Holy Spirit at all.

Finally, John agrees with pre-Christian sources that the indwelling Spirit is not to be understood as having a direct moral influence, but rather an indirect one through the prophetic message. This is made clear especially in the lengthy discourse including chapters 13-17. Too often statements from these chapters have been universalized for all Christians, when it is clear that Jesus was talking to the twelve about the circumstances soon to come upon them after his departure. But even for the twelve the Holy Spirit was not to empower them for righteousness, but rather their reception of the Spirit was contingent upon their living righteously.

CHAPTER SIX

THE HOLY SPIRIT IN HEBREWS, I-II PETER, AND JUDE

Since Paul is the most ambiguous, and therefore the most difficult, writer in the NT to interpret, I shall leave his contribution until last. In this short chapter we shall look at a miscellaneous collection of NT writings. The first is a sermon known as The Book of Hebrews.

In 2.1-4 the writer can be found comparing the old religious economy of Judaism with the new movement begun by Jesus. His first comparison had to do with the Law of Moses, having been given to Moses by angels, and the Gospel, delivered by Jesus.

> Therefore we must pay the closer attention to what we have heard, lest we drift away from it. ²For if the message declared by angels was valid and every transgression or disobedience received a just retribution, ³how shall we escape if we neglect such a great salvation? It was declared at first by the Lord, and it was attested to us by those who heard him, ⁴while God also bore witness by signs and wonders and various miracles and by gifts of the Holy Spirit distributed according to his own will.

In line with rabbinic thought the writer ascribed to the OT inspiration mediated by angels. Hence, Christians should be especially attentive to the gospel. For if the OT, which was given through the instrumentation of angels, was sanctioned by God's wrath, then the salvation dispersed by the new covenant is even more deserving of attention. This is the case because it was declared by Jesus the Lord (not just angels) and was attested (confirmed) to others by signs, wonders, miracles, and gifts distributed by the Holy Spirit. Here we have a clear association between the Holy Spirit and miracles and also an allusion to the witness role of the Spirit which has surfaced already in other NT writings. The miracles served as a witness to the truth of the Gospel.

We also saw in the rabbinic writings that when the scriptures were meant sometimes the phrase "the Holy Spirit" was used. We see this several times in The Book of Hebrews, which is itself written in the style of a rabbinic sermon. For example, in He. 3.7-9 the writer quotes Ps. 95.7-11 but introduces it with the phrase, "as the Holy Spirit says." Similarly, in He. 10.14-17 a quotation of Je. 3.33-34 is introduced with, "And the Holy Spirit also bears witness to us; for after saying, ..." Then in He. 9.6-9 a description of Levitical rituals is taken as an indication by the Holy Spirit "that the way into the sanctuary is not yet opened as long as the outer tent is still standing." In other words, the laws of Leviticus are the words of the Holy Spirit. Since the rabbis held that the scriptures were inspired by the Spirit and that they also were a living organism (thus addressing the concerns of all of God's people at all times), they regarded the Scriptures as a way that the Holy Spirit spoke to them directly (very much like some conservative Christians regard the NT today). The author of the Book of Hebrews seems to view the matter in the same light. We can thus infer from this perspective that spiritual blessings attributed to the Spirit are not always to be understood as coming from the Spirit directly. If the Spirit inspired the writers of the scriptures, then anything we might derive from the scriptures might also be said to have been derived from the Spirit. We have seen already, and shall see especially in the writings of Paul, that many wonderful things are ascribed to the Spirit, things like joy, fellowship, love, comfort, and even salvation, but we do not have to conclude from this that these things come about by a direct work of the Spirit from the inside (from the internal working of the Spirit) but might just as well be said to come about indirectly and externally by the working of the Spirit through inspired persons, such as the apostles and early church leaders.

In He. 6.5 we find a reference to those who have become partakers of the Holy Spirit, that is fellows, or fellowshipers, of the Holy Spirit, yet these same persons had committed apostasy. There is nothing in the context to clarify this term, but it is listed with such things as being enlightened, tasting the heavenly gift, and tasting the goodness of God and the powers of the age to come. Apparently, these are ways of referring to the gospel. These people have come to know the truth of the gospel, they have been saved from their sins, they have come to know God's word, and they are expectant with regard to God's kingdom. Partaking of the Holy Spirit could simply mean that these people are in fellowship with God, but, given the heavy association, not only here but also in all the other literature, with miraculous powers, it would seem that the author here is referring to their having received these powers. So, his aim is to point to the utter inconsistency of their having received the Holy Spirit with its attendant powers and their having apostasized. So, once again we see that having such powers would be of some spiritual encouragement, as would knowing God's word, being saved, and having Christian relationships, but it would appear from this passage that there is nothing uniquely powerful about the indwelling Spirit as far as successful Christian living goes.

There are several unusual references to spirit in Hebrews, some of which might refer to the Holy Spirit. One of these occurs in 9.13-14.

> For if the sprinkling of defiled persons with the blood of goats and bulls and with the ashes of a heifer sanctifies for the purification of the flesh, [14]how much more shall the blood of Christ, who through the eternal Spirit offered himself without blemish to God, purify your conscience from dead works to serve the living God.

The best clues to the meaning of "the eternal Spirit" come from some similar references in Hebrews. For example, the writer in 5.9 speaks of "eternal salvation" and in 6.2 of "eternal redemption." By these he probably meant being saved from sin (as opposed to physical and temporal salvation and redemption), but more informative examples come from the context of chs. 8-10. Here the writer lays out a comparison between the Levitical sacrifices and the sacrifice of Jesus upon the cross, the main point being that the former were physical while the latter was nonphysical, or spiritual. As high priest Jesus serves in the true tabernacle, one not set up by man (8.1-2). The Levitical priests were only a copy or a shadow of the true one (8.5, 10.1), or heavenly one (9.23-24). Their sacrifices could not "perfect the conscience of the worshiper" but dealt only with "regulations for the body imposed until the time of reformation" (9.9-10), whereas Jesus' sacrifice actually secured "an eternal redemption" (9.11-2) and an "eternal inheritance" (9.15), which perfected his disciples (10.14). Whereas the Levitical priests entered the holy of holies (9.7), Jesus entered heaven itself (9.24) and sat down at the right hand of God (10.12). They reentered every year, but Jesus once and for all time (9.25-26, 10.11-12). So, even though it is possible to think of Jesus' sacrifice somehow being offered through the Holy Spirit, the more likely interpretation is that Jesus offered a spiritual sacrifice, not a physical one, and one which secured an eternal consequence, as opposed to one that would require continual reiteration.

Another interesting and unusual reference to spirit is found in He. 10.28-29.

> A man who has violated the law of Moses dies without mercy at the testimony of two or three witnesses. [29]How much worse punishment do you think will be deserved by the man who has spurned the son of God, and profaned the blood of the covenant by which he was sanctified, and outraged the Spirit of grace?

I have found the phrase "spirit of grace" only once *(The Testament of Judah* 24.3, cf. *Sourcebook)*, where it was predicted that the Messiah would himself receive an outpouring of the Spirit, after which he would pour out the spirit of grace on the Jews. From the context it appears that it is similar to Joel 2.28-32, which was taken by the rabbis to declare that the Messiah would bestow miraculous gifts at the dawn of the new age. However, in He. 10 it is difficult to determine from the context what might have been meant. Since the Spirit of grace is outraged, it would appear to be personal, not a principle or an attitude. The phrase could be a reference to God, or it might refer to the Spirit. Perhaps, as we saw in Ac. 5.3, since the Holy Spirit was so active in the early church, those who were disobedient were seen to be disobeying or being rebellious to the Holy Spirit. Hence, the writer of Hebrews was saying that for a Christian to fall away from the faith was to outrage the Holy Spirit.

We now turn to First and Second Peter.

Peter began his first letter by addressing it to those "chosen and destined by God the Father and sanctified by the spirit for obedience to Jesus Christ." The question therefore arises as to whether Peter meant that they were sanctified by the Holy Spirit or whether *their* spirits had been sanctified. The grammatical construction allows for either. In 1.15-16 Peter called upon his readers to be holy (the same as sanctified). Then in vs. 22 he reminded them that they had had their souls purified by their obedience to the truth. These ideas are parallel. So, the latter interpretation is to be preferred because of the context. However, even if the first of the two interpretations above is chosen, we are still not told *how* the Holy Spirit sanctifies one. Peter called upon his readers to live sanctified lives. Perhaps the Spirit accomplished this through the gospel and Christian prophets. There is no mention of an indwelling here and no need to supply one. Neither is the work of the Spirit (if it is the Spirit) automatic, since Peter called upon his readers to yield themselves to holy living, implying their acquiesence. So, this is probably not a passage about the Holy Spirit at all.

Later in the chapter (1.10-12), Peter, encouraging his readers to continue in the faith, reminded them of how important the gospel really was. Even the OT prophets, who prophesied about these events, did not see them as clearly as did these early Christians. The OT prophets even inquired as to what was "indicated by the Spirit of Christ within them." Now, the phrase "Spirit of Christ" will come up twice in Paul's writings (one of which could refer to the Holy Spirit, the other probably not), but it has already occurred in Ac. 16.7, where it was closely connected to the Holy Spirit's guiding the apostles' missionary efforts. However, even there it could refer to an actual visionary appearance of Jesus (cf. Ac. 18.9-11 and 23.11). But here in I Pt. it is very clearly identified with the Holy Spirit in its prophetic capacity. Similarly, in 1.12 Peter referred to "the things which have now been announced to you by those who preached the good news to you through the Holy Spirit sent from heaven, things into which angels long to look." He was referring to the inspired apostles preaching the gospel to them. In fact, this last sentence might even answer our question with regard to I Pt. 1.2, that is, if the Holy Spirit sanctified Christians, how did he do it? The answer then would be through the inspired preaching of the apostles.

Next in I Pt. we come to 3.18, where it says that Jesus was "put to death in the flesh but made alive in the spirit; in which he went and preached to the spirits in prison, who formerly did not obey, when God's patience waited in the days of Noah, during the building of the ark, ..." Commentators are divided as to whether Peter meant that Jesus was made alive, that is resurrected, by the Holy Spirit, or that in spirit form he was made alive and went to the spirits in the nether world. One problem with the first interpretation is how we are to understand Jesus going into the nether world *by the Holy Spirit.* The more likely interpretation is the second, indicating a contrast between flesh and spirit. In the flesh Jesus died, but in spirit form he entered the realm of the dead. In the Palestinian Judaism of Jesus' day "spirit" was sometimes used for the dead who roam the earth, for the spirit of man which roams about while the body sleeps, or for the bodiless spirit which waits in an intermediate state after death for the resurrection. Also, in the gospels we encountered "spirit" as ghost; for example, when Jesus appeared after his resurrection, his disciples thought he was a spirit (Lk. 24.36-39). So, perhaps Peter was saying that Jesus as a bodiless spirit went to the underworld prison. Add to this the plausible view that Jesus went there between his crucifixion and his resurrection (Cf. Ac. 2.26), and the latter interpretation is even better established.

Finally, in I Pt. we come to 4.14: "If you are reproached for the name of Christ, you are blessed, because the spirit of glory and of God rests on you." The text is somewhat corrupt, but this is the preferred reading. It contains an unusual phrase with regard to the spirit, but it probably refers to the Holy Spirit. Jesus had promised his disciples the Holy Spirit would speak for them in times of persecution (Mt. 10.20, 24.19-20, Mk. 13.11, Lk. 12.12, 21.14-15, Jn. 14.26, and 16.7-11). So Peter could be telling his disciples here not to be intimidated when they are persecuted for the name of Christ, since by that very name they had come to possess the Holy Spirit, not only a privilege in itself but also the source of inspiration by which they answered their critics.

Our only passage from II Peter has to do with the inspiration of OT prophets (II Pt. 1.20-21):

> First of all you must understand this, that no prophecy ever came by the impulse of man, [21]but men moved by the Holy Spirit spoke from God.

The context here has to do with false prophets in the church and how they will destroy the Body. The writer begins with a contrast between the message of the apostles and that of the false teachers. Unlike the latter, Peter and the others were eyewitnesses (1.16). Moreover, the apostolic word is even better than that; it is on the level of OT scripture. Such prophecy was not merely the ingenious ideas of human beings, no matter how enlightened, but rather the result of the direct work of the Holy Spirit sent into the prophet by God. Incidentally, it is hard to ignore the very close similarity between the above quotation and the words of Philo with regard to the same subject quoted in Chapter Two above.

Our last excerpt in this chapter comes from Jude 19-21. Again, the subject is the danger of false prophets in the Christian fellowship.

> It is these who set up divisions, worldly people, devoid of the Spirit. [20]But you, beloved, build yourselves up on your most holy faith; pray in the Holy Spirit; keep yourselves in the love of God; [21]wait for the mercy of our Lord Jesus Christ unto eternal life.

Jude therefore denied the false prophets' claim to have been inspired by the Holy Spirit; they were in fact devoid of God's Spirit. This is not a reference to the character of God, but rather to the indwelling prophetic Spirit.

In contrast, Jude encouraged his readers to grow, to stay in the love of God, to be patient, to work with those in doubt, and to pray in the Holy Spirit. What does it mean to pray in the Spirit? "In the Spirit" is translated "inspired" in Mt. 22.43, Mk. 12.56, Lk. 2.27, and Ac. 19.21. In Lk. 10.21 Jesus rejoiced in the Holy Spirit, but his rejoicing took the form of prayer. Also, the group prayer in Ac. 4.23-33 was probably an instance of inspired prayer. So, this instance in Jude is as well a reference to inspired prayer. There will be more on this subject later, but now to summarize.

In this miscellaneous collection of NT literature there were seven very clear references to the Holy Spirit. Of the seven, six were certainly associated with the miraculous: working signs or prophesying, whether in spoken form or written form. However, eight ambiguous instances remain. Of these eight one was associated with prophecy and two with the miraculous. Two simply make no associations so as to enable us to determine what was meant exactly. The other three were almost as unclear. For example, when I Pt. 1.2 said that we are sanctified by the Spirit (or in the spirit), if it referred to the Holy Spirit then it probably referred to the process of one heeding the word of truth so that his soul is purified (1.22), or sanctified (1.15-16) through Christian preachers with the gospel. When I Pt. 4.14 speaks of the spirit of grace resting upon someone, it might very well refer to charismatic gifts. And finally, the false prophets were devoid of the Spirit (Ju. 20) in the sense that they were not inspired. Once again, then, the clear statements about the function of the Holy Spirit connect that role with signs, wonders, miracles, prophecies, and the inspiration of scriptural prophecy. Then, recourse to the principle of letting the clear passages interpret the ambiguous ones leads us to interpret the latter as also having to do with miracles and prophecy.

CHAPTER SEVEN

THE HOLY SPIRIT IN THE LETTERS OF PAUL

I have saved Paul until the last for two reasons. Most commentators believe that Paul has the fullest doctrine of the Spirit, having emphasized certain aspects which the other biblical writers perhaps did not; and secondly, Paul is the most ambiguous of any of the others on this subject, though most commentators would not agree with this second point. With all of the background material from the OT, intertestamental Judaism, the secular Graeco-Roman world, and the other NT documents, perhaps we can understand Paul better than we could in isolation. However, as in all efforts at interpretation, some attention to some principles will be very helpful. For example, we should be careful about going beyond the texts or reading into the text. Going beyond the text means forcing it to say things which it does not say. This means that in some instances we might have to settle for some ambiguity. Reading into the text means importing ideas into the interpretation which the author could not, or very likely did not, know about himself. For example, importing twentieth century western social-psychological issues into an interpretation of Paul's letters would be a very dubious enterprise. Similarly, unless there are overwhelming and explicit reasons for doing otherwise, we should restrict ourselves to those ideas available to the author in his day. Another important principle to remember is that the NT writers were addressing specific issues occasioned by circumstances in their day. How their words might apply to later generations under entirely different circumstances is a totally different matter. After all, no NT passages were written directly to us today.

So, with those things in mind let us take a look at the main texts in Paul which have to do with the Holy Spirit. The Book of Hebrews aside, thirteen NT documents are ascribed to Paul. Though I personally think that all of them were written fairly closely together, we shall take them in their probable chronological order.

First, there is the very important section of Galatians, chapters 3-6. In this letter Paul was concerned about Gentile Christians being forced under the Law of Moses by overzealous Jewish Christians. Paul's main point in the first two chapters of the letter was that his practice of baptizing Gentiles without imposing upon them the Law of Moses was approved of God, already accepted by the leaders of the church, and in keeping with the logic of grace. Part of his argument against this had to do with the fact that his audience had received miraculous gifts when they became *Christians,* not when they accepted Judaism (3.1-5).

> O foolish Galatians! Who has bewitched you, before whose eyes Jesus Christ was publicly portrayed as crucified? ²Let me ask you only this: Did you receive the Spirit by works of the law, or by hearing with faith? ³Are you so foolish? Having begun with the Spirit, are you now ending with the flesh? ⁴Did you experience so many things in vain? -- if it really is in vain. ⁵Does he who supplies the Spirit to you and works miracles among you do so by works of the law, or by hearing with faith?

Paul's argument would fall short if his readers could not tell very clearly exactly when they had received the Spirit. But they could do so, because the reception of the Spirit was indicated by the acquisition of miraculous powers, as is explicitly stated in vs. 5. Here again we see the witness aspect of the Spirit in the apostolic period. The obvious signs of the Spirit served to confirm Paul's doctrine that faith in Jesus, without entering the Jewish covenant, was sufficient.

Paul then went on to argue that it is men of faith in Christ who are the true sons of Abraham, because those who rely on their obedience to the Law of Moses are under the curse of that law.

> [13]Christ redeemed us from the curse of the law, having become a curse for us -- [14]for it is written, "Cursed be every one who hangs on a tree" -- that in Christ Jesus the blessing of Abraham might come upon the Gentiles, that we might receive the promise of the Spirit through faith.

Paul understood the gift of the Spirit to be the blessing which God promised the true sons of Abraham. There is, of course, another way to understand the phrase, "the promise of the Spirit." It could mean either the promised Spirit or that which the Spirit promised. The Greek construction will allow either, so the context must decide between them. Looking at the context, 3.29-4.7, we find Paul asserting that since the Galatian Christians were Christ's possession then they were God's sons, if sons then heirs, and because they were heirs God had sent the Spirit of His Son into their hearts. So, if that is a reference to the Holy Spirit, then it is the Spirit which was promised, not something which the Spirit promised.

Since these Gentile Christians were now heirs of Abraham, not even the Law of Moses could abrogate that fact. Furthermore, that would mean that the Law was merely a temporary aspect in God's scheme of salvation. It was like a tutor for a child, temporary and preparatory. Now that a system based on faith in Christ had come, all people, both Jews and Gentiles, could become Abraham's offspring by faith in Jesus as the Christ (3.15-29).

As we saw above, at this point Paul stated that God had "sent the Spirit of his Son into our hearts, crying 'Abba! Father!'" (4.6). Several things in this context seem to me to indicate that here Paul was referring to the phenomenon of inspired prayer. First, he had already described the function of the Holy Spirit as the work of confirming the truth of the gospel. That work consisted of miracles, or literally signs, and inspired prayer would certainly be a sign. As the New English Bible has it: "To prove that you are sons, God has sent into our hearts the Spirit of his Son, crying, 'Abba! Father!'" Secondly, as some scholars point out, "crying" probably connotes inspiration (cf. eg., I Enoch 71.11, cited in Chapter Two above). Also, in the NT, when Elizabeth prophesied, it was with a loud cry (Lk. 1.41; cf. Ac. 2.18 and 4.24). And thirdly, calling God "Abba" was not a natural thing to do. In Aramaic it meant "Daddy," a very familiar and casual appellation, one which would normally be offensive to the hearers when addressed to God, unless the users had been inspired in its use.

Next in Galatians Paul expressed his perplexity over their acquiescence to the Judaizing teachers (4.8-20), after which he presented an allegory, comparing the Law of Moses to Ishmael and Christianity to Isaac (vv. 21-31). Ishmael, Paul said, was born according to the flesh, while Isaac was born according to the Spirit. At least two important points emerge from this comparison. First, Ishmael's birth was according to the flesh in that it came about by the will of a man, namely Abraham. Isaac's birth was according to the Spirit in that it was engineered by God, prophesied beforehand, and miraculously effected. Secondly, the comparison shows that for Paul to speak of certain things being by the Spirit means that it is entailed in this new covenant, the one generated and guided by the Holy Spirit, not by the written text of the OT. In other words, the Holy Spirit was associated in the mind of Paul with a new covenant, a point relevant to Paul's next reference to the Spirit.

In Chapter Five Paul appealed to the Galatian Christians to resist the pressure of the Judaizing teachers for them to come under the Law of Moses. Instead they should take the path of sonship and freedom. For through the Spirit there was the hope of being justified from sin (5.5). Paul was here speaking of two covenants again, two systems. The Law of Moses was written. This new movement was Spirit-directed through the apostles and prophets. Paul therefore was continuing his comparison of the system of justification based on the written law to the system of justification based on the gospel message presented by the Spirit-inspired leaders of the new Christian movement. By accepting the gospel believers were being justified through the Spirit. One of the reasons this comparison is difficult for us today is that we often think of Christianity in terms of a system based on a written text, namely the NT; but in Paul's day the only authoritative written text was the Torah, and that made the prophetic movement of Christianity suspect.

In vv. 16-26 we encounter Paul's Spirit/flesh dichotomy. We have encountered the two terms before, but not always as opposites. Most significantly, John compared flesh with spirit, where the two were more like qualities than entities. We also have the examples of dualistic language in the background literature. For example, in the Dead Sea Scrolls there were two principles, one of light and one of darkness, engaging in combat behind the scenes with each other for moral control. Similarly, there were the two impulses taught by the rabbis. So, there are two possibilities for Ch. 5 of Galatians. Either Paul was contrasting two realms, the spirit versus the flesh, or he was contrasting the Holy Spirit with man's physical nature. The latter is more likely, though, for in Ga. 3.3 Paul contrasted the Holy Spirit and the flesh. I have to conclude, then, that walking by the Spirit meant living in accordance with the teachings of the Spirit as delivered by prophets in contrast to walking according to the flesh, which meant living according to human impulses.

In 5.18 Paul spoke of being led by the Spirit. The idea of being led by the Spirit is rare in the NT (cf. Ro. 8.14). The subject is more current on the lips of modern Christians than it was in the NT texts. We do not have to infer an inner leading here either. From the context it is highly plausible that Paul was referring to Christians being led by the Spirit through the teachings of the inspired apostles.

In 5.25 Paul said, "If we live by the Spirit, let us also walk by the Spirit." As we just saw, walking by the Spirit obviously meant living a righteous life, so then, to live by the spirit must refer to salvation. Christians had come to receive eternal life through the Spirit (cf. 5.5 and 6.8). In other words, Paul was saying that since they had been justified by the inspired gospel message, they should also live by the Spirit's moral injunctions. This verse also shows how walking by the Spirit was anything but automatic; Paul had to remind his disciples of their commitment to discipline the flesh and to yield to the Spirit's demands.

Another early Pauline statement on the Spirit occurs in I Th. 1.4-7.

> For we know, brethren beloved by God, that he has chosen you; ⁵for our gospel came to you not only in word, but also in power and in the Holy Spirit and with full conviction. You know what kind of men we proved to be among you for your sake. ⁶And you became imitators of us and the Lord, for you received the word in much affliction, with joy inspired by the Holy Spirit; ⁷so

that you became an example to all believers in Macedonia and in Achaia.

We are fortunate in this case, however, to have a commentary on this passage by Paul's own hand, namely 2.13:

> And we thank God constantly for this, that when you received the word of God which you heard from us, you accepted it not as the word of men but as what it really is, the word of God, which is at work in you believers.

It appears that Paul meant that when he and his fellow missionaries preached the gospel to the Thessalonians it was attended by miracles, the witness of the Holy Spirit, and that they were therefore duly convinced that Paul's message was from God.

Another interesting passage from I Th. is 5.19-20: "Do not quench the Spirit, do not despise prophesying, but test everything; . . . ." In intertestamental Judaism the inspiration of the Holy Spirit was often associated with fire, and even in Greek writers like Plutarch we can read discussions on the quenching of the Spirit. In light of this it seems that Paul was warning his readers that prophetic powers had to be treated properly, or else they could be extinguished. Prophecy was to be respected, however what the prophets said still had to be tested.

We now come to Paul's letter to the Romans, thought by most to contain the most central statements of the NT on the Holy Spirit. In that great section which begins with chapter five and ends with chapter eight, Paul stated that God's love had been poured into their hearts through the Holy Spirit which had been given to them (5.5), but that statement is best understood in terms of what Paul would say later.

In chapter 7 Paul took up a criticism that his teachings were derogatory with regard to the Law of Moses.

He used the analogy of marriage to state (and the analogy is not perfect) that through Christ they, his Jewish audience, had died, thus severing the marriage bond they had had with the Law of Moses. This death therefore freed them to marry another, that is, Christ, and to bear fruit to God through righteous living. No longer did they serve God under the oldness of the letter but under the newness of the Spirit. In modern parlance we have a letter-of-the-law/spirit-of-the-law distinction; but, even though there was a distinction in Roman law between the words of a law and the intent of that law, there is no evidence that that was what Paul meant here. There is no evidence that the words "spirit" and "letter" were used by the Romans for that distinction, and more importantly, such a distinction would not fit the context here. The distinction Paul made is again the distinction between a system based on an actual written law and one based on Spirit-led teachers, that is between Judaism and Christianity.

Paul then went on to defend himself against the charge that he had disparaged Moses' Law by saying that it encouraged sin. No, the Law itself was not bad; it was just that sin could use the Law to get human beings to break it (7.7-12).

Then arose the related question, namely, whether the Law was responsible for people's spiritual death, their separation from God. No, again. Paul contended that the responsibility lay with human beings and the weakness of the flesh. The Law is spiritual; human beings are fleshly. The responsibility for sin and spiritual death is ours. In saying this, Paul once again referred to the spirit/flesh (or, spiritual/fleshly) dichotomy, which did not necessarily have anything to do with the Holy Spirit. As we saw in our survey of intertestamental Judaism, there was the Jewish view that human nature is bifurcated by two impulses, one good and one evil, one internal and one of the flesh. The spirit here is aligned with the heart, while the flesh is aligned with the passions of the physical body. Paul's point was that it is the latter which leads us to violate God's law (7.13-25).

We now come to a passage deeply concentrated on the concept of the spirit (8.1-17).

> There is therefore now no condemnation for those who are in Christ Jesus. ²For the law of the Spirit of life in Christ Jesus has set me free from the law of sin and death. ³For God has done what the law, weakened by the flesh, could not do; sending his own Son in the likeness of sinful flesh and for sin, ⁴he condemned sin in the flesh, in order that the just requirement of the law might be fulfilled in us, who walk not according to the flesh but according to the Spirit. ⁵For those who live according to the flesh set their minds on the things of the flesh, but those who live according to the Spirit set their minds on the things of the Spirit. ⁶To set the mind on the flesh is death, but to set the mind on the Spirit is life and peace. ⁷For the mind that is set on the flesh is hostile to God; it does not submit to God's law, indeed it cannot; ⁸and those who are in the flesh cannot please God.
>
> ⁹But you are not in the flesh, you are in the Spirit, if the Spirit of God really dwells in you. Anyone who does not have the Spirit of Christ does not belong to him. ¹⁰But if Christ is in you, although your bodies are dead because of sin, your spirits are alive because of righteousness. ¹¹If the Spirit of him who raised Jesus from the dead dwells in you, he who raised Christ Jesus from the dead will give life to your mortal bodies also through the Spirit which dwells in you.
>
> ¹²So then, brethren, we are debtors, not to the flesh, to live according to the flesh -- ¹³for if you live according to the flesh you will die, but if by the Spirit you put to death the deeds of the body you will live. ¹⁴For all who are led by the Spirit of God are sons of God. ¹⁵For you did not receive the spirit of slavery to fall back into fear, but you have received the spirit of sonship. ¹⁶When we cry, "Abba! Father!" it is the Spirit himself bearing witness with our spirit that we are children of God, ¹⁷and if children, then heirs, heirs of God and fellow heirs with Christ, provided we suffer with him in order that we may also be glorified with him.

Our first point is that Paul contrasted two "laws," two systems, one of the Spirit of life in Christ Jesus, the other of sin and death (8.2). Paul averred that his Roman brothers and sisters had been delivered from the latter, not by anything which they had done, but rather by what God had done for them through Christ (vv. 3-4). However, Paul's aim in chs. 7 and 8 was to show that the gospel was antagonistic neither to the Law of Moses nor to the requirement of righteous living. Indeed, those who walk by the Spirit succeed in living up to the Law far better than those who walk by the flesh.

It is at this point that a certain ambiguity emerges in Paul's argument. Paul in ch. 8 could have been referring to the Holy Spirit as opposed to the flesh or to the spirit side of man as opposed to his carnal side. It is commonly noted that the letter to the Romans is very similar to the letter to the Galatians. Under our discussion of select verses from Galatians we found a flesh/spirit distinction with the call for Christians to walk by the latter. There we decided, because of the context, that Paul was referring to Christianity as a new religious movement inspired and led directly by the Holy Spirit as opposed to Judaism (probably rabbinic Pharisaical Judaism) and any other system which emphasized the physical. Paul could have been making the same distinction here in Romans.

However, the context of Ro. 7-8 suggests the alternative interpretation. Ch. 7 revolved around the spirit/flesh distinction in human nature, the two impulses which pull human beings in one direction or the other. Paul probably means the same in ch. 8. Hence, his statements so far would not be about the Holy Spirit at all, but rather about the inner moral conflict within human nature.

Further still, we could say that Paul in both Galatians and Romans slipped from one sense of spirit to the other, but that is still saying that Paul was ambiguous.

The ambiguity continues in vv. 5-9. Paul explained how those who set their minds on things of the spirit found themselves in harmony with God's will, while those who set their minds on the things of the flesh became hostile towards God's commandments. Yet, for our purposes it is still difficult to tell whether Paul was referring to the Holy Spirit or to man's spiritual side.

The next verses, 9-11, provide some interesting twists. First, Paul told his congregation that they were not in the flesh but in the spirit, that is, if the Spirit of God dwelled in them. The latter reference sounds like the Holy Spirit. Paul also referred to an indwelling; that sounds like the personal indwelling of the Holy Spirit, as we have found it in so many other passages. Then in vs. 11 he spoke of the Spirit of the one who raised Jesus from the dead dwelling in them and giving life to their mortal bodies. After all, in the parallel passage in Ga. 4.6 Paul said that God had sent the Spirit of his Son into their hearts, crying "Abba! Father!" and there we decided that it was the Holy Spirit inspiring prayer. However, the intervening verses sound different. Paul referred to this spirit as "the Spirit of Christ." He also talked of this circumstance as "having Christ in you." So, it is possible that Paul was still talking about a state of mind, as he was in the previous verses. The spirit of God, then, could have been the mind of God.

Vs. 9, "Any one who does not have the Spirit of Christ does not belong to him," has become one of those overworked passages, which is commonly used to prove 1) that the reception of the Holy Spirit is involved in, if not identical with, conversion; and 2) that the indwelling of said Spirit is the *sine qua non* of Christian discipleship. There are several problems with these hasty conclusions, though. First, there should be some question, as we have already noted, as to whether this is a reference to the Holy Spirit at all. Second, even if this is the Holy Spirit, nothing was said about the point at which Christians received it; it would not have to be simultaneous with the conversion process. Third, though this verse might be taken to say that all Christians sooner or later received some special gift of the Spirit, it would not follow that this should be understood as a pattern of Christianity for all time. Lastly, and most importantly, point 1) above would contradict the patterns we found in the Book of Acts. This verse is just one statement among so many in the NT and should not be taken alone as the decisive statement on the role of the Spirit.

Vv. 12-17 are a summary and are therefore somewhat repetitive of the thoughts already expressed. However, vs. 15 speaks of one's being led by the Spirit of God. Though this could be an awkward reference to God's nature, it makes more sense to think of one's being led by the Holy Spirit. We came across this idea in Ga. 5.18, but it does not occur in this sense anywhere else in the NT. In both passages it appears in a contrast between the Spirit and the Law of Moses, where the latter is somehow understood as being approached in a fleshly sense. It would further seem, then, that Paul in Romans was referring to this new religious movement, begun by Jesus but carried on through the prophetic work of the Holy Spirit. Being led by the Holy Spirit, therefore, meant believing and following the prophetic teachings of the early Christian prophets.

Later, Paul stated that when he and his Christian fellows cried "Abba! Father!" it was the Spirit himself bearing witness with their spirits that they were children of God. Again this is the Holy Spirit. We saw the same thing in Ga. 4.6-7, where we took it to refer to inspired prayer. By inspiring the early Christians to refer to the Father with the unusual appellation of "Abba" the Holy Spirit was functioning in its familiar witness role.

The remainder of Ro. 8 rounds out the points Paul outlined in ch. 5. In fact, Ro. 8.18-39 is a commentary on

5.3-5, where Paul had said that suffering produces a hope in Christians which will not be disappointed inasmuch as the Holy Spirit had poured the love of God into their hearts. In 8.18-25 Paul restated that very point.

Then in 8. 26-27 we find,

> Likewise the Spirit helps us in our weakness; for we do not know how to pray as we ought, but the Spirit himself intercedes for us with sighs too deep for words. [27]And he who searches the hearts of men knows what is the mind of the Spirit, because the Spirit intercedes for the saints according to the will of God.

Creation groaned, Christians groaned, even the Holy Spirit groaned. Paul to some degree explained the Spirit's groaning: it was meant to help the disciples in their weakness, the weakness being not knowing what to pray for. In this context, Paul probably meant that the Spirit would help the disciples when they were emotionally disabled. To some extent Paul's words remind us of Jesus' in Jn. 14-16. There Jesus warned his disciples of impending persecution, but promised to send them the Holy Spirit as a helper. The Spirit's help in John, though, was primarily in terms of prophecy and miracles. In Romans only prayer is mentioned. Furthermore, the Spirit helped by interceding with (lit.) unuttered groans. It interceded in behalf of the disciples and in accordance with the will of God. How did this occur? One suggestion has been that, as the rabbis taught, Paul was encouraging the disciples at Rome by reminding them that the Spirit was always before the throne interceding for the saints. They could not hear this intercession, but they could infer what the Spirit was saying from OT passages. A more plausible explanation, though, is that Paul was referring again to inspired prayer. This really would have been encouraging to these Christians, especially at a time of persecution. What was unuttered was not the words of the Spirit, but the groans. Paul was telling the Christians there that they could infer the sympathetic groans of the Spirit from the inspired prayers they heard.

Paul then concluded this section of his letter with an explanation of how the Spirit had poured the love of God into the hearts of his readers (cf. 5.3-5). It was nothing mystical or mysterious; it was simply the gospel: if God had not spared his own Son, then who could effectively bring accusation against the ones who had accepted the atonement of Jesus' blood (8.28-39)?

In conclusion on Ro. 7-8, it must be said that it is quite possible that many of the statements about spirit are about that spirit-side of human nature, that part which harbors the impulse for good, and not about the Holy Spirit at all. And even if most of them are about the Holy Spirit, it does not follow that this is a normative passage, that is, a passage telling us something eternal about Christians for all time. Rather, these remarks might have been about the work of the Spirit at that very special time during the church's infancy when Christians had special miraculous powers. Neither would it follow that these passages are about a personal inward leading of the Spirit. Paul was contrasting the nature of this new movement as led by the Spirit through prophets with what Judaism had become at the hands of many of the rabbis of his day, a rather legalistic and externalistic exercise.

Finally, when Paul spoke of the Holy Spirit pouring love into the heart (5.5, 15.30), as he did about joy (I Th. 1.6), and when he spoke about God giving life through the Spirit (Ro. 8.11) or people by the Spirit putting to death the deeds of the body (8.13), Paul was simply speaking of the impact of the message of the Holy Spirit through the Christian prophets of his day. This can be seen more clearly in our last look at Romans. In 14.17 Paul spoke of "righteousness and peace and joy through the Holy Spirit." Then in 15.13 he said, "May the God of hope fill you with all joy and peace in believing, so that by the power of the Holy Spirit you may abound in hope." How did all of these blessings come to the respective persons through the Holy Spirit? Just a few verses later Paul answered this question. He went on to say that he, as a God-appointed minister to the Gentiles, had been very bold with them, because he wished to present them to God as an acceptable sacrifice, "sanctified by the Holy Spirit" (15.14-17). He was, in fact, proud of his work among them, how he had won their obedience "by word and deed, by the power of signs and wonders, by the power of the Holy Spirit" (vv. 18-19). In other words, the above blessings had come to the Gentiles through the gospel, which was both inspired and confirmed by the Holy Spirit. The power was not so much internal as it was through signs and wonders manifested to them. Moreover, whereas the Law of Moses was powerless to save (8.3), the gospel was quite powerful (1.16).

We now turn to some other significant statements on the Spirit as found in Paul's extant correspondence with the Christians at Corinth.

The first of these letters can be easily divided into the separate problems which Paul addressed. The first problem had to do with divisions in the Body over various estimations of various preachers. Paul explained to the Corinthians how many Jews and Greeks had rejected the gospel because the preachers and the message did not often appeal to human categories of greatness, like power and erudition. As for his own presentation, Paul was quite honest (2.3-5).

> And I was with you in weakness and in much fear and trembling; and my speech and my message were not in plausible words of wisdom, ⁴but in demonstration of Spirit and power, ⁵that your

> faith might not rest in the wisdom of men but in the power of God.

This word "demonstration" occurs only once in the NT but several times in secular Greek. The basic meaning has to do with proof. In fact, the lexicon gives the following on the above verse: "proof consisting of the possession of the Spirit and power" (Arndt and Gingrich, p. 89). Paul's whole point was that his power to convince the Corinthians had had nothing to do with his own personal charm but rather with the miracles he had performed. He wanted their faith to rest on God's power, not on any compelling human features.

Paul did not deny that he had a wisdom to impart, just that it was not the wisdom of man, which was so tied to the glorification of human attributes. The story of Jesus was not compelling from the human point of view, thus it had not been readily accepted; but the wisdom behind it, God's wisdom, had been revealed to Paul through the Spirit (2.6-9).

> For the Spirit searches everything, even the depths of God. [11]For what person knows a man's thoughts except the spirit of the man which is in him? So also no one comprehends the thoughts of God except the Spirit of God. [12]Now we have received not the spirit of the world, but the Spirit which is from God, that we might understand the gifts bestowed on us by God. [13]And we impart this in words not taught by human wisdom but taught by the Spirit, interpreting spiritual truths to those who possess the Spirit.

Since the gospel would never have been dreamt by unaided human intelligence, it had to have been revealed. Just as one cannot know another's thoughts, one cannot know God's unless He reveals them to him. However, Paul claimed, that is just exactly what God had done through the Spirit, and the revelation had been in terms of explicit verbal and propositional information.

The last phrase in 2.13 is admittedly controversial. The phrase is made up of only three words in Greek and admits of several possibilities: interpreting (or comparing, or combining) spiritual things (or persons, ideas, words, etc.) to (or with, for, or by) spiritual things (or persons, ideas, words, etc.). The context has to do with how people can know the mind of God. If the prior paragraph is determinative, then Paul was saying, "interpreting spiritual ideas in spiritual words." But if Paul was leading into his next point, which had to do with the spirituality of the hearer, then Paul meant, "interpreting spiritual ideas to spiritual persons." Either is possible, but because of some minor grammatical constructions, I lean toward the first.

Paul then went on to say that the problem in reception was the state of the hearer's heart. The unspiritual (fleshly or worldly) man could not see past his own biases, while one who was humble was open to God's will. There is nothing in this whole passage about one's possessing the Holy Spirit. Paul and the apostles could be said to have possessed the Spirit since they were inspired transmitters of God's message, but no statement is made here about the necessity of one's having the Spirit in order to understand the gospel, even though such a view is very old, having been stated first by Origen in the third century.

We now come to a new passage. In I Co. 3.16-17 Paul referred to the corporate church as God's temple, housing God's Spirit. This is not a reference to an individual indwelling. As we saw in the OT, for the Spirit to dwell in *some* individuals meant that the Spirit dwelt in Israel as a whole. Paul here was probably making a point about the importance of the church based on the presence of God's miracle-working Spirit in it.

But the most important passage on the Spirit in the letters to the Corinthians is I Co. 12-14, a three-chapter section which deals with spiritual gifts, such as healing, prophecy, and tongue-speaking. Paul began by pointing out that there was a variety of such gifts, all bestowed by the same Spirit, so that they should all be employed harmoniously (12.1-11).

> [12]For just as the body is one and has many members, and all the members of the body, though many, are one body, so it is with Christ. [13]For by one Spirit we were all baptized into one body -- Jews or Greeks, slaves or free -- and all were made to drink of one Spirit.

First, Paul was saying that as a result of the recent extraordinary work associated with the gospel of Christ those who had been baptized (in water) in the name of Christ had been baptized into one body, namely, the one church. Secondly, Paul was saying that in addition to having been baptized by one Spirit into the one Body of Christ, the above persons had also experienced that one Spirit, that is, they had received miraculous gifts.

Of course, my conclusions are not without disagreement. I Co. 12.12-13 is understood by some to conflate water baptism in the name of Jesus Christ for the remission of sins with Holy Spirit baptism, thus making the reception of the Holy Spirit part of the conversion process. Admittedly, the phrase "by one Spirit" could be translated "in one Spirit," so that this would be a reference to baptism in the Holy Spirit. Furthermore, in most cases of baptism in the Holy Spirit (there are six others), the Holy Spirit is the element, not the agent. However, the argument against this conflation is much stronger. To begin with, such a view runs counter to all the examples in Acts, where Holy Spirit baptism is quite separate from the conversion process; and since Luke and Paul were close coworkers, it is doubtful that they would differ so sharply about conversion and the Holy Spirit. Secondly, the immediate context argues for an instrumental relationship to the Spirit, that is, Paul meant "by," not "with." Earlier in the chapter Paul spoke of the various spiritual gifts, which came "by" (vs. 3), "of" (vs. 7), "through" (vs. 8), "according to" the Spirit (vs. 8), and "as the Spirit wills" (vs. 11). Thirdly, Paul had elsewhere spoken of people being justified or sanctified by the Spirit (II Th. 2.13, Ro. 15.16-20, and I Co. 6.11), where he meant that people had come to believe the gospel and to be saved as a result of seeing the attendant signs and wonders. And finally, this verse is not like the other six: the whole point here was to say that people had been baptized by *one* Spirit, where the other passages were not emphasizing the unifying element of baptism. Indeed, compare the parallel statement in Ga. 3.27-28:

> For as many of you as were baptized into Christ have put on Christ. [28]There is neither Jew nor Greek, there is neither slave nor free, there is neither male nor female; for you are all one in Christ Jesus.

So, Paul's point in I Co. 12.13 was that as a result of the work of the Holy Spirit in the inspired preaching of the gospel the Corinthians had become unified by being baptized (in water) into the one Body of Christ.

To emphasize the unity of Christians even further Paul went on to compare the church to a human body, in which it is so important that all of the individual parts work together for the good of the whole. Hence, all the various spiritual gifts were to be used for building up the church (12.14-30).

The famous chapter on love which comes next continues this thought. There Paul argued that the spiritual gifts were temporary, serving a special purpose during the infancy of the church, but that the day would come when the church would grow out of them. What would abide throughout all the ages in which the church continued on the earth were faith, hope, and love, and love was the greatest of these because, unlike faith and hope, it would continue even into eternity (13.1-13).

Then in ch. 14 Paul applied the principle of love to the practices of spiritual gifts. Overall, his message is clear: use your gifts for the edification of the Body. However, there are some intriguing statements. In 14.2 Paul stated that for one to speak in tongues with no interpreter was to utter "mysteries in the Spirit." Of course, Paul was referring to miraculously acquired language skills here. But in 14.12 he said, "For if I pray in a tongue, my spirit prays but my mind in unfruitful," and in 14.32, "the spirits of prophets are subject to prophets." And as we saw in rabbinic Judaism, the prophet's spirit could mean the prophetic faculty, so that Paul was saying that he prayed by inspiration on occasion but his mind did not understand what was said because it was in a foreign tongue (cf. Moses's spirit in Nu. 11. 17 and Elijah's spirit in II Ki. 2.15).

So, I Co.12-14 is a very important passage on the Holy Spirit, but it deals with the proper use of miraculous gifts for the building up of the Body in love.

We now come to the second letter to the Corinthians. The first significant statement is 1.21-22; but before discussing it we should notice that Paul makes statements like this one three more times, and we should take them together. So, II Co. 1.21-22:

> But it is God who establishes us with you in Christ, and has commissioned us; [22]he has put his seal upon us and given us his Spirit in our hearts as a guarantee.

II Co. 5.5:

> He who has prepared us for this very thing is God, who has given us the Spirit as a guarantee.

Ep. 1.13-14:

> In him you also, who have heard the word of truth, the gospel of your salvation, and have believed in him, were sealed with the promised Holy Spirit, [14]which is the guarantee of our inheritance until we acquire possession of it, to the praise of his glory.

Ep. 4.30:

> And do not grieve the Holy Spirit of God, in whom you were sealed for the day of redemption.

The similarities among these texts are clear, and combined they make the following points. God had placed a seal on Christians, that seal being His promised Holy Spirit. The reception of the Holy Spirit in their hearts amounted to an earnest (down payment or guarantee) toward the future possession of an inheritance. The reception of the Holy Spirit followed their coming to faith in Christ and entering Christ. Moreover, this seal served to motivate these early Christians.

The promise referred to above is very likely the promise we discussed under Lk. 24-Ac.2, which was the eschatological baptism of the Holy Spirit, with its attendant signs and wonders. This baptism served as a seal, that is, as a stamp of approval upon this new movement of Christianity. People throughout the world had stepped out on faith, and the baptism of the Holy Spirit confirmed their faith. It also served to convince nonbelievers.

In my *Sourcebook* I have a fuller discussion of the meaning of the word "guarantee," but suffice it here to say that the baptism of the Holy Spirit was a pledge of God's promise to include Christians in the eternal kingdom. Now, I happen to hold to a rather minority view that the second coming of Christ occurred at the destruction of Jerusalem in 70 A.D., at which time the new messianic kingdom was finally and fully established. It is far too complicated a view to set out here, but it is my conviction that the period between the crucifixion and the fall of Jerusalem was a transitional period between two great ages. Those who weathered the extreme hardships of that period entered the messianic age and thus received their inheritance. The gifts of the Holy Spirit aided and encouraged Christians during that very difficult time. So, just as when one fulfilled his promise he retrieved his pledge (cf. Gn. 38.17-20), the baptism of the Holy Spirit was a temporary phenomenon, meant to assure early Christians that their hopes were not misplaced.

A second significant passage in II Co. is chapter three, where we find that Paul's opponents had apparently charged him with arrogance. Others had required letters of recommendation. Paul's response was that the Corinthians themselves constituted Paul's letter of recommendation, not a literal letter, but a letter written on hearts, instead of in ink, by the Spirit of God. Apparently, some of Paul's opponents were legalistic Judaizers, enamored with the Law of Moses. Paul's point was that his ministry was not characterized by legal erudition and especially not by a stilted adherence to Jewish traditions; rather it was characterized by the work of the Holy Spirit, which had resulted in the changed lives of the Corinthian Christians.

Paul then hastened to add that none of this had come from his own abilities, but that by God's grace he had been given his role in promulgating a new covenant, one inspired and confirmed by the Holy Spirit. As a result, he was filled with hope, confidence, encouragement, and boldness. Paul stated that his sufficiency was from God, "who (had) qualified (the apostles) to be ministers of a new covenant, not in a written code but in the Spirit; for the written code kills, but the Spirit gives life" (vs. 6).

Paul had contrasted letter and Spirit before (Ro. 2.29 and 7.6). In each case the contrast was between one who followed the Law of Moses and something else, one an inward law and the other ambiguous. So, here Paul seems to have been contrasting two systems, two eons, one characterized by the Law of Moses and the other by the workings of the Holy Spirit.

However, an interpretive problem familiar to many readers of Paul is that on the one hand he speaks highly of the Law of Moses, and on the other hand he speaks derogatorily, II Co. 3 being one of the latter instances. I would suggest that in the former instances he was actually referring to the old law, but that in the latter he was speaking of a perverted, legalistic version of Judaism of the Pharasaic sort. This would explain Paul's pejorative comments in this passage, where he refers to the old law as a "dispensation of death" (vs. 7). Hence, Moses' Law had great splendor (vs. 7), but at the hands of the Jews it had become something spiritually lethal. The new dispensation, though, the one of the Spirit (vs. 8), would therefore have even greater splendor.

Vv. 12-18 are especially interesting. In these verses Paul continued his contrast between the two dispensations. The former, Paul said, was approached in such a way by the Jews that they were hindered from seeing the truth of the gospel, but by turning to Jesus that hindrance would be taken away. Paul then made a play on Ex. 34.14, where it says, "whenever Moses went in before the Lord to speak with him, he took the veil off, until he came out; . . . ." Instead of the word "Moses" Paul said "a man," thus making an allegorical use of the text in Ex. Paul also twice identified "the Lord" with the Spirit, so as to make the point that one is liberated from the blinding effects of Jewish legalism by turning to this new movement of the Spirit. However, this is still allegory; and one should be very careful about extracting certain Trinitarian implications from such a use of an OT text.

One should also be very careful about reading this passage as if Paul were talking about some inner work of the Spirit upon the individual, liberating him (miraculously) from sin and spiritual blindness. No, the comparison here was between two systems. The work of the Spirit was constantly presented in an eschatological fashion which contrasted the features of an old system which was ending and a new and greater system just beginning. As always, we need to be wary of reading twentieth century American "new age" ideas into a first century text about the gospel.

Another category of "Spirit" occurrences in Paul's letters would include connections between the Spirit and fellowship (II Co. 13.14), joy in the Spirit (I Th. 1.6, Ro. 14.17), love in the Holy Spirit (Ro. 5.5), worshiping God in spirit (Ph. 3.3), and even sanctification in the spirit (II Th. 2.14, Ro. 15.17, I Co. 6.11). It is highly questionable in some of the cases whether it is even the Holy Spirit which is under consideration, but rather the spirit as opposed to the flesh. But even if these things are connected to the Holy Spirit in these passages, nothing is said as to just what that connection was. For example, the fellowship of the Spirit could refer to the working partnership of the Spirit with the early Christians through the miraculous powers bestowed upon them. Moreover, the reader should also question whether the relationship with the Spirit is corporate or individual.

We next come to some passages in Paul's letters to the Ephesians and the Colossians. I want to take them together because, as it is often pointed out, the two letters are so very similar that they serve to interpret each other.

The first relevant passage is Ep. 2.17-3.7 with the companion passage of Co. 1.24-27, where Paul dealt with God's great plan for unifying all peoples into one family through the gospel. Whether Jew or Gentile, they "both have access in one Spirit to the Father" (Ep. 2.18), built together into a temple for God in the Spirit (Ep. 2.22). But as was unusual for Paul, he proceeded in Ep. 3.1-7 to explain himself rather clearly, where he stated that the above unity had been accomplished through the gospel which had been revealed to the apostles through the Spirit. As we have seen before, when Paul attributed certain spiritual blessings to the work of the Spirit he meant that they had been effected through the Spirit-inspired message of the gospel (cf. Ep. 6.17). In fact, in Ep. 4 Paul repeated the same point. In this passage Paul entreated them to pursue precious Christian unity, and he mentioned seven bases of that unity; but then he went on to say expressly that Jesus had bestowed upon the church miraculous gifts for the "building up of the body of Christ until we all attain the unity of the faith . . ." (2.13).

Another interesting pair of passages is Ep. 5.15-20 and Co. 3.16-17, where Paul encouraged his readers to avoid the foolish debauchery of the world and instead to "be filled with the Spirit, addressing one another in psalms and hymns and spiritual songs, singing and making melody to the Lord with all your heart." I would suggest that this passage is about inspired singing in the assemblies of early Christians. All the heretofore instances of persons being filled with the Spirit have had to do with miraculous powers, especially prophecy, and two of these have contrasted being filled with wine with being filled with the Spirit (Lk. 1.15 and Ac. 2.15). This contrast has served to show that the disciples were under the control of something, only not wine. (However, this is not to say that being under the control of the Spirit was ecstatic or drunken-like, since Paul explicitly calls the latter debauchery). Similarly, in Ep. 6.18, where Paul enjoined his readers to "pray in the Spirit," he was encouraging them to pray inspired prayers in the assemblies and by so doing to encourage the other disciples by the words of the Spirit.

We end this study of Paul's writings on the Spirit with two excerpts from the Pastorals. The first is the well-known statement about the inspiration of scripture, II Ti. 3.16-7. The word here for inspired is a very rare form of the word for spirit, but it does occur in two other places. One instance is in a Greek passage referred to as "The Sentences of Pseudo-Phocylides" where inspired wisdom is said to be very much superior to human wisdom. Also, in Hermetic literature the word referred to information received through direct revelation from a divine being. So, at least this much can be said, by "inspired scripture" Paul was referring to something revealed directly by God.

Finally, we come to Ti. 3.5-7 where Paul said that God had

> saved us, not because of deeds done by us in righteousness, but in virtue of his own mercy, by the washing of regeneration and renewal in the Holy Spirit, ⁶which he poured out upon us richly through Jesus Christ our Savior, ⁷so that we might be justified by his grace and become heirs in hope of eternal life.

This passage teaches two things. First, sinners were saved, along with God's mercy and baptism, by a renewal of the Holy Spirit. Several times in Paul we have come across such statements (Ga. 5.25, I Co. 6.11, 12.13, II Co. 2.13, and Ro. 15.16). Paul also mentioned renewal elsewhere (Ro. 12.2, II Co. 4.16, and Co. 3.10) and enjoined disciples everywhere to engage themselves vigorously in the process. Some of the passages we have examined already, and we found reason to see the work of the Spirit as functioning through the message of inspired prophets. The same would probably be the case here.

The second relevant teaching in this passage is that the Holy Spirit had been poured out on Paul's readers. That would suggest the baptism of the Holy Spirit and would support our interpretation under the first point, namely, that Paul was referring to the manifestation of miraculous gifts, which were used for the preaching of the gospel and the edification of the disciples.

This brings us to the end of our study of Paul on the Spirit. About half of the time when Paul refers to the Holy Spirit he means miraculous gifts, such as speaking in unlearned languages, effecting healings, and especially prophesying, but the biggest problem with Paul on this point is his ambiguousness. Of course, in the case of ambiguity the only reasonable thing to do is to use the clear passages to interpret the unclear ones. To do otherwise would be to open the door to just about any possible interpretation out there in the imagination. So, the most plausible understanding of Paul foots squarely with the views of the other biblical writers, namely, that the personal indwelling of the Holy Spirit empowered persons with miraculous gifts for the purpose of confirming the word of the gospel. It is true that Paul associated the Spirit with salvation and morality a bit more than do the other writers, but only in an ambiguous way. There is no need to attribute to Paul some view of the Spirit as working internally in the lives of every Christian in every age, bringing him to salvation and empowering him for moral improvement. It is a more likely interpretation to say simply that Paul attributed everything in Christianity to the Spirit because he was impressed by the eschatological significance of the miracles which were so prominent in the early church.

CHAPTER EIGHT

CONCLUSIONS

I propose that the nature and function of the Holy Spirit is fairly clear and simple. As it has been stated before in this book repeatedly, the Holy Spirit is that aspect of God which is associated with acts of power, and when dwelling in a person it produces miracles, especially the miracle of prophecy. The critical factor in this conclusion is the overwhelming similarity among precedent usage in background materials. When a term is so unified in its use, a very strong case must be made for any new interpretation. Furthermore, writers such as Luke are so clear in their association of the Holy Spirit with miraculous powers that it is obvious they are continuing to refer to the work of the Holy Spirit in the same way as did their literary predecessors. I recognize that the interpretation of this book is not a popular one (it is even rare among scholars) and not a very inviting one, but we must always endeavor to let texts say what they say.

In this last chapter I wish to bring together some of the various themes developed in the earlier chapters. First, there is no difference to be made among various terms like "the baptism of the Holy Spirit," "to receive the gift of the Spirit," "to receive the Spirit," "the Spirit being poured out," "to be clothed by the Spirit," "to have the Spirit come upon someone," and other such phrases. They are used interchangeably in the NT. However, terms such as "spirit" or "spiritual" need not have any direct connection with the Holy Spirit

A study of the Holy Spirit almost always raises questions about the Trinity, a subject with a history far to large for this book, but a few remarks might be made. I do not see why we should say that the Holy Spirit is a separate person from God the Father and the Son. The Holy Spirit in the Bible is more of an aspect of the one God. "The Spirit of God" or "the Holy Spirit" is a term which the biblical writers used when they wanted to speak of God's power, especially as it became immanent in the physical creation. It is significant to me that the idea of a binity (the notion of a two-person Godhead) does not seem to come up with the reading of the OT. Instead, the Holy Spirit becomes a third person only after reading the NT back into the old, especially since Jesus during his earthly ministry clearly was a person distinct from his Father in heaven. The Father, the Son, and the Holy Spirit, then, represent three ways in which the one God has manifested Himself in the world: as the Father through the creation, as the Son through Jesus, and as the Holy Spirit through prophecy and miracles.

In my *Sourcebook* I treat the subject of miracles with greater attention to detail than I have in this book, but let it suffice here to treat only the matter of the temporary employment of miracles. That they were primarily a first century phenomenon (as far as Christianity is concerned) is not as clear as one might want, but there seems to be a connection between them and the eschatological shift brought about by Jesus the Messiah. The miracles indicated both the last days of Judaism as the religious movement of God and the inauguration of the messianic movement. Once that transition was made the miracles would cease. However, debate over the duration of miracles should be one of the easiest religious questions to resolve. Miracles are obvious; if they were to occur at any time, biblical prooftexts would not be necessary.

Next, the Holy Spirit, especially the idea of the baptism of the Holy Spirit is not a part of conversion. Certainly, the gospel, being inspired by the Spirit, is necessary to conversion, but the indwelling of the Spirit is not. There is no indication in the NT that one must have the indwelling Spirit in order to be open to or to understand the gospel message. There is no indication that the Holy Spirit causes or directly works on a person's heart in order for him to come to Christ. The baptism of the Holy Spirit is the reception of miraculous powers, not conversion, and could occur before or after one became a saved disciple of Jesus. Neither is the baptism of the Holy Spirit connected to water baptism, the rite which, according to the NT, brings one into the Body of Christ.

Similarly, throughout the Bible, there is no connection made between the indwelling Spirit and moral improvement. In fact, even prophets appear to be just a part of their own audiences. They enjoyed no specially privileged position, and many who had the Spirit did poorly.

The same could be said about things like hope, joy, comfort, fellowship, and strength, things which are sometimes said to be a product of the Spirit. The NT writers do not teach that such things come about by a direct influence of the Holy Spirit from within the believer, rather a stronger case can be made that, even though such things come from the Spirit, they come about indirectly through the influence of the prophetic message. There is a tendency in American society today to look to quick, automatic, effortless, individualized, and inward remedies to our problems. The answers are from God, certainly, and the answers have been mediated to us through the Holy Spirit, but they exist for us in the Word. When we internalize the

Word, pray for God to work in the circumstances of our lives, draw strength from the fellowship of other believers, and work consistently and patiently toward change, God's answers to our problems can be realized in our lives.

However, it has often been argued that Paul is an exception, that he plowed new ground theologically and made a direct connection between the work of the Holy Spirit and both salvation and moral empowerment. But the connection is only apparent. Paul had been steeped in rabbinic Judaism. When he came to Christ his whole world changed. There was a new and profound movement afoot, given impetus and guidance by the work of the Holy Spirit in the apostles and prophets of the church. So, instead of attributing spiritual things to the Torah, he began to attribute things to the Spirit. He was contrasting two epochs. Paul was often clear in his references to the Spirit and meant the same thing as did the other biblical writers, but too often he was ambiguous, allowing for creative interpretations. Sometimes it is quite unclear as to whether he was even referring to the Holy Spirit at all, rather than to a distinction between the flesh and spirit sides of human nature. Furthermore, one of the most remarkable aspects along this line in the works of Paul is that on those occasions when he was addressing morality and the things which give impetus to a righteous life he says nothing about the Spirit. If he sought to give us a new perspective on the ethical impact of the indwelling Spirit, he strangely ignored all the best opportunities to do so. So, the case for an inventive view of the Spirit on the part of Paul is weak at best, and the most plausible interpretation is that Paul was simply contrasting the oldness of rabbinic Judaism with the newness of this Spirit-led movement of Jesus.

One of my concerns in making this study was to discover to what extent the Spirit functions in a personal, inward, and mystical way in the lives of believers. I found that it does not do so. There is no teaching about an inward leading by the Spirit, nor about an operation of the Spirit which directs the disciple toward the center of God's will, whatever that might be. Even the prophets themselves had no particular advantage at understanding the message of the Spirit which inspired them; to them also the message was a propositional revelation coming to them from without. One of the great contributions made to the world by the Judeao-Christian tradition is the emphasis it has placed on objective principle-driven morality. I confess my concern that viewing the work of the Spirit in a personal and subjective way might lead many away from the heart of this tradition and toward a fleshly religion.

Another concern that I had upon making this study was that we not allow our modern American consumerism to affect our understanding of the Spirit. We are characteristically concerned about what things can do for us. Our first questions usually have to do with what is in Christianity for us, but the early disciples received the Spirit not for themselves but for others. They were equipped with miraculous (mainly prophetic) powers for carrying out the mission of Jesus to an unsaved world. Because of the directly supernatural guidance they received from the Holy Spirit we today are blessed richly with every spiritual gift.

Finally, I might add that an unnecessary reaction to the thesis of this book is that the above view of the Holy Spirit implies that Jesus' disciples are alone in the world, abandoned to fend for themselves helplessly against the treacherous spiritual enemies of God's Kingdom. It is unnecessary, because God has always worked to protect, lead, and strengthen His people, and not only through the Word, but through circumstances in our lives and through the church. Jesus' disciples are not alone, just because the Holy Spirit functioned at particular times in the form of miracles and not at others. The biblical texts are replete with information and examples of how God works in the lives of His servants, but they are not necessarily found in those texts which mention the Holy Spirit and so would need to be treated in yet another book.